ISLAM & NIHILISM:
MY POISION & MY CURE

NIHILISM & ISLAM:
MY POISON & MY CURE

YUSUF PONDERS

SAPIENCE
PUBLISHING

Copyright © 2023

All rights reserved. No part of this book may be reproduced in any form or by any electronic or mechanical means including photocopying, recording and information storage and retrieval systems—except in the case of brief quotations embedded in critical articles or reviews—without the permission in writing from the author or publisher.

Sapience Publishing. First Edition, 2023.
www.sapienceinstitute.org

Typesetting by Imran Rahim • Etherea Design
Book Design: UmmahGraphics

Contents

PREFACE	1
Who Am I & Why Do I Care?	3
Introduction	11
PART ONE: BEGINNING TO UNDERSTAND NIHILISM	15
The Philosophy of Nihilism	17
The Importance of Nihilism	19
Nihilism's Relevance to Goals and Values	23
A Higher Value Undermining Itself	25
PART TWO: THE CAUSES & EFFECTS OF NIHILISM	29
The Rise of "Post-Truth"	31
Societal Exhaustion	33
Overwhelmed by Overabundance	35
Nihilism as a Sickness	39
Truth & Techno-Hypnosis	43
Society, Obligation & Duty	45
A Fractured Society	51
Morality, Meaning & Leaps of Faith	55
The Nihilist Yearning	61
PART THREE: OVERCOMING OBSTACLES	65
What Obstacles?	67

Why Believe in the Divine?	69
No Empirical Evidence?	71
Too Many Gods & Religions!	75
On the Wisdom of Old	81
More on Leaps of Faith	87
On Finding Balance	93
PART FOUR: ISLAM AS AN ANTIDOTE	97
The Final Step	99
Recommending Prevention and Cure	101
Post-Truth and Epistemic Nihilism	105
Overcoming Pessimism & Instilling Hope	109
Combatting Scepticism and Moral Nihilism	115
Patience, Contentment & Perseverance	123
Duty & Responsibility	127
A Solid Foundation for the Human Being	131
Conclusion	141
BIBLIOGRAPHY	143

*For my daughter.
May Allah keep her firm upon Islam
and make her a blessing for the Ummah.*

*For my mother, brother, and sister.
May Allah guide them and those they love
to the religion of Islam.*

بِسْمِ اللَّهِ الرَّحْمَٰنِ الرَّحِيمِ

In the name of God, the Merciful, the Giver of Mercy
All praise and gratitude are due to God,
the Lord of everything that exists.
May God's peace and blessings
be upon His final Prophet
and Messenger,
Muhammad.

PREFACE

Who Am I & Why Do I Care?

Many people around the world suffer from depression, and some opt for suicide to escape their anguish. Through my work on nihilism, I have had numerous individuals reach out to me and express their suffering from these issues. Nihilism is a very personal topic for me. It›s not only a lived experience, but I have also witnessed the suffering it has inflicted on those close to me who have fallen prey to the same anguish. I know what it feels like to look out into the world and see nothing but dust, to stare into a black abyss, to lay your suffering and hardship out in front of you, and to see no rhyme or reason as to why it exists, or why you had to go through so much pain. I, too, have felt my heart being crushed within my chest under the weight of my despair due to the apparent meaninglessness of all my experiences. I have suffered from severe depression and social anxiety, which led me to run away and later to isolate myself for many years. My motivation for wanting to tackle this subject is connected to my story, and so, I wanted to share it with you first, so that you can understand me as a writer and what brought me here, to discuss this incredibly depressing subject.

So, who am I? I was born in the North of England, in a small town on the border of Manchester. My mother came here from Poland when she was three years old, and my father moved here from Glasgow after he met my mother. They had three children: first me, then my brother, and then my sister. We were raised as Catholics, baptized, received Holy Communion, went to a Catholic school, Church, and Polish Sunday school. We grew up on a council estate and were far from rich.

My mum was a great provider. She worked a lot in restaurants, doing double shifts and making sure we had what we needed. My dad, not so much. He was a heroin addict who was constantly in and out of prison. He came from a rough place, and I suppose this motivated him to want to toughen me and my brother up. He made us watch horror movies from a very young age. Everything from The Exorcist, The Omen, to The Children of the Corn. When he was around and not incapacitated from the heroin, he was obsessed with "making us brave". My mother, in contrast to him was very nurturing, loving and kind. This would cause tension as my dad believed this would make us too soft. The world was a dangerous place, and we needed to be men!

When I was nine years old, my dad passed away from a heroin overdose and three days later my little sister was born. April 1st, 1998, a date that is imprinted in my memory. The day my dad died, and the day that my tension with God began. My brother and I were in our beds pretending we were still asleep. It was a school day, and we figured that everyone had just forgotten. We could hear a lot of commotion downstairs, so we hid under our sheets, barely able to contain our laughter. The excitement of potentially getting a day off school filled us with glee. Our family from Glasgow had come down to visit us, and we were excited at the thought of getting to spend more time with them.

At 9:00am, when we knew we had officially missed school registration, my brother and I skipped down the stairs with big smiles on our faces ready to embrace our day off with the family. However, when we got to the bottom, we noticed there were a lot of strangers in the house. With my family were policemen, paramedics, and my neighbours. I was confused. I couldn't quite figure out what was happening. I recall seeing my pregnant mother crying, and with one of my aunties we were taken away from the living room so we couldn't see what was happening. We sat on the stairs and my mother was unable to speak because of the tears. She had to tell us something but couldn't quite say it. Eventually someone said:

"*Your dad has passed away.*"

I'm sure other things were said, but to be honest this is all I can remember. I remember not really knowing how I was supposed to react, and just looking at my mum being distressed. I wasn't quite sure how to process it. It didn't feel real. We were told one of my uncles was driving down from Glasgow to take us to Scotland, and that we needed to go pack some clothes.

I went to go and get ready, and while I was packing and I was on my own, not thinking about how I was supposed to react, reality began to sink in. I began to get angry at God. I recall complaining to Him and asking Him why he would do such a thing to us. My dad was 33 when he died. As I write this now, I am the same age he was when he passed. It didn't make sense to me.

We took his body to Scotland to be buried next to my grandmother, his mum. I recall attending the wake and having the opportunity to stand by my dad's body, holding his cold hands and speaking to him. I remember asking him to wake up and kissing him on his cold forehead. I remember the strange smell of the chemicals they put on dead bodies. I refused to leave his side for a while, and people came in and out the room to give their respects.

The priest came to give a sermon by the coffin, and I recall looking at my mum, holding my little sister who had just been born not long after my dad had died. I remember them lowering the coffin into the ground, and I remember screaming at them not to do it. I remember it all very vividly. The colours, the people, the place, the emotions. It wasn't an easy thing to experience. We then continued for many years after this, to experience much more death in our family, and with close friends. We had loss because of alcoholism, suicide, drug abuse and old age.

Eventually we stopped going to church and I went to a secular school. Religion became a distant thing to me. I consumed media and played games which often mocked religious tendencies. My only experience with religious people was "the crazies" that would stand on boxes screaming bible quotes. As time passed, I became more and more atheistic and began to believe that religion was no more than a tool to control the masses.

The idea that religion was for crazy people was reinforced on September the 11th, 2001. I recall watching the news very intently and being shocked at what I was seeing. How could anyone do this? How could anyone go so far? At this point I was certain there was no God and continued to live my life as such.

From here I went headfirst into a materialistic lifestyle. I worked and saved money so I could spend it on material things. I smoked weed, obsessed over girls, spent thousands on clothes and aftershaves. I became a social chameleon with many different groups of friends from diverse social groups. My life was just work then play, work then play, work then play.

Eventually I made some new friends who were Muslim, and this led me to engaging more and more with religion. After reading the Qur'an and engaging in many discussions with them I temporarily moved away from hard atheism and became more agnostic for a time, but still found it difficult to let go of my distaste for religion. I think at one point I may have even said it's very possible that a God exists. But I didn't see myself committing to a religion like Islam at the time because there were too many restrictions, and it was very controversial. I had lots of things I wanted to do, and being a Muslim would be something that would completely get in the way of that, so I never took the step.

I continued in my materialistic ways but couldn't ignore how pointless it all felt. Science fascinated me, and I loved watching shows like "Through the Wormhole" which only increased my appreciation of the beauty and vastness of the universe, while at the same time realising my own insignificance. Life continued to have its ups and downs. I, and the people around me, continued to go through difficulties, suffering, pain, and trauma. I read the news about all the crazy things that were happening around the world. I couldn't help but keep asking: What's the point of all this?

Life was monotonous, and my depression crept in like a dark cloud. I was increasingly dissatisfied with life, and no number of worldly things offered any solution. I became ever more uncomfortable around my friends. Life was repetitive, frustrating, and boring, so I decided to run away. I saved up as much as I could and went travelling around Asia for 18 months. I sold all of my belongings and owned nothing other than my tiny backpack and its contents.

In this time, I stayed and worked in several Buddhist temples, met people from all over the world from every religious background, and got into many discussions about the meaning of life, death, God, and religion. I had no obligations and no place I needed to be. When I got bored or sick of a place, I'd pack up and leave. For 18 months, life was a constant adventure. I lived on a tropical Island and ran a bar, worked with wild animals like tigers, lions, and bears, went to full moon parties, wild camping, scuba diving and couch surfing. I lived more in these 18 months than I had done in my entire existence before that.

As amazing as all these experiences were, it wasn't enough to keep the nihilism I had been experiencing at bay. Paradise could quickly turn to hell in the blink of an eye. I could fall in love with a place, and in one minute it would quickly reveal its hidden dark underbelly. I witnessed many terrible things and spoke to some terrifying people.

The complexity of life and the world gradually revealed itself to me in more detail. I saw the good, the bad, and the ugly. I was struggling to make sense of it all. I had all this information in my head about all these different belief systems and opinions about what the purpose of life was (that is if it had any purpose). I was struck with a sudden realisation. There is just too much information. There was absolutely no way I could sift through all of this and process it all before I died. So, I surmised, if there was too much to process for all of mankind, how could I ever imagine I could do this by myself? There was too much chaos, too much flux. One minute, someone would seem like a great person, next minute you find out something very dark about them, or you witness or become victim to something dreadful. Another time you meet someone terrible, only to find out they're going through some great difficulty which forces you to feel empathy for them. Just when you think you have something understood, something else happens to completely shake the confidence you had.

Eventually my savings dried up, and I had to return home. The depression slowly began to creep back in. I had spent so long in a certain mode of being, with no commitments and no responsibilities, only to be thrown back into the "normal" world again. I found it difficult to acclimatise, and eventually fell into severe depression and suffered from acute social anxiety. I had plenty of friends but cut them all off. I deleted my social media and withdrew into a shell. I watched documentary after documentary, and witnessed over and over what the worst of humanity could do. I was exposed to dark corners of the internet where I saw humans doing terrible things. I couldn't help but ask, what on earth is going on? What is all of this for? What's the point?

In my isolation, I slowly and gradually sank, deeper into an abyss. I was in its grip. And at its deepest point, when my life seemed the darkest, and I felt completely alone with my thoughts and pain, unable to communicate or share it with anyone, I recalled many of my discussions with people around the world about religion and God. In a moment of desperation, I prayed to something I wasn't even sure existed. I asked generally, to whatever is out there, whatever it is that's in control of all of this, whatever it is at the very top of existence, for help and guidance. I wasn't quite sure which God I was praying to, or whether He, or it, or whatever it was, could hear me, but I prayed, nonetheless.

My Godless state had taken me to an abyss of utter meaninglessness. There was a conflict inside of me that did not make sense, between my need for meaning and the apparent inability of the world to offer it to me. I remember in my darkest moment, it felt like my identity melted away. All the things I thought I was, all my "achievements", all dissolved. I was left as nothing, as a nobody. Reality had sunk in. I was no one special, my life was nothing significant. I had no allegiance to anything. My only concern at this point, was truth, and I had lots of questions.

I began my journey through the different major religions again. I investigated Buddhism, a religion I was very fond of, and continued to go to Buddhist centres in Manchester. I read about the life of Buddha and his teachings amongst other things like practising meditation. I also investigated Hinduism and new age spiritualists like Ram Dass, Eckhart Tolle, and many others. I was becoming more and more open to the ideas of spirituality and had some minor experiences that began to make me more sceptical of the atheistic/agnostic mindset. I felt myself making a transition.

I'll be honest, Islam was not at the top of my list. It was an incredibly controversial religion, and the idea of being a Muslim felt like too much effort. However, I wanted to give each religion a fair shot, so I began to read the Qur'an again and investigate the life of the Prophet Muhammad ﷺ and his companions. I was reading books, watching videos, and listening to talks. At this point I invested all my time into these things and just exposed myself to as much information as I could consume and process. The more I did this, the more I became convinced of Islam, above everything else.

This was frustrating for me because it was scary. I could probably have entered any other religion and not have gotten much grief about it. Especially when I was dabbling in Buddhism, people didn't seem to have a problem with that. But Islam was different. Islam receives a lot of negative media attention, and Muslims have a bad reputation. The thought of having to tell people I had become among this group frightened me.

It would have been incredibly convenient if I could just find a reason, any reason, to consider it false. Then I could avoid all the controversial conversations, avoid all the commands about halal and haram, avoid the obligations of prayer and fasting. If I could just follow something easy like Christianity or Buddhism, where for the most part there isn't really any obligations beyond what I "fancy". That would have made life so much easier.

However, the more I investigated the more I became convinced of Allah's existence, of the Oneness of God, of the Divine Authorship of the Qur'an, and of the Prophethood of Muhammad ﷺ. The more I went over it in my head, the more I confirmed to myself that each one of these propositions had a big tick next to it, and that I found the counter claims in other religions or ideologies to be unsatisfactory in comparison. I was essentially a Muslim in belief, but I found it difficult to take that step to expressing that belief outwardly. The more I thought about it, the sillier I felt. I was all too familiar with death and knew my end could arrive at any moment. What would I say to Allah if that day arrived, and I did not testify to the truth and take shahada? If I am asked if I believed in His existence, in the Qur'an, in Muhammad ﷺ, my answer to all these questions would be Yes. But what would my answer be when I am questioned about why I did not submit and become a Muslim? Upon reflection, I had to admit that the ultimate reasons would be because I was a coward and feared what people would say to or about me; I was lazy and did not want the commitments involved; I was a fool and couldn't see my beliefs through. What kind of excuse would this be? It became clear to me that to fear and love the world and the things it contained more than Allah was foolish, especially considering at this point I believed in it. So, I declared my testimony of faith and became a Muslim.

I kept it secret for many years, while I continued my journey of seeking knowledge. I studied with scholars, I read books, I went to university and continued to engage in dialogue on the subject. With each passing year I became increasingly convinced, strengthening my convictions even more. I was also amazed to witness how it completely turned my life around. Whereas before I was falling into a sense of nihilism, now it seemed impossible to be held by its grip. Islam had successfully filled my life with meaning and purpose that was unmatched by anything I had ever experienced. Everything I ever went through had a purpose to it, good or bad, and all that really mattered was how I dealt with it. Islam offered a guidance and a way of being. It helped me understand right from wrong and gave clear restrictions from the many things that harmed me in my youth, and many of the others who were around me. It gave me structure and discipline, and it helped me to develop knowledge and a connection with Allah. The more I learned about Him and His religion, the more I loved Him. Eventually, establishing the prayer became easy for me. If I ever miss a prayer (which is rare), I feel like I have lost something precious. I get excited for Ramadan. I have love for people and have formed amazing bonds with them after such short periods of times simply because we share a love for Allah and His messenger ﷺ. Islam gave me brotherhood and a community to be a part of. It gave me my life back.

It was like life was without colour, and then suddenly, I could see all the different hues in vivid brightness. My depression all but vanished, and my passion for life and engaging with people was reinvigorated. Where once I was sinking into an abyss, consumed by nihilistic tendencies, Islam had freed me from that. It was strange, because I still suffered, I still experienced loss and pain, but now, there was a sweetness that accompanied it. There was a reason for all the difficulties in life, and as down as I feel sometimes, I never lose hope. I hold firm to the rope of Allah, above the abyss.

My studies at university were in Philosophy, and my dissertation was about nihilism and the meaning of life. I spent a long time grappling with the works of Nietzsche and other existential philosophers who spoke about this subject in depth. I began to develop my insight into the issues that gave rise to nihilism on a societal level, and the consequences of it having its grip on a people. Having experienced it on a personal level and spoken to many people dealing with the same issues, it has become a topic close to my heart. I took it upon myself to try to contribute towards helping people overcome nihilism. I believe Islam is the answer to this, and in this book, I wish to demonstrate how that is the case.

Introduction

In this work, I intend to make clear, a few of the motivating factors that give rise to nihilism and its consequences. I then hope to direct the reader to practical solutions which will help keep nihilism at bay; or alternatively, point towards a path which will help those who already suffer from it, to overcome it. I will do this in multiple stages. I will begin by focusing mainly on addressing nihilism as a sickness. The latter part of the book will focus more explicitly on Islam as a solution to nihilism and overcoming obstacles and accepting it genuinely as an antidote.

I will take the following steps. First, I will define nihilism. I will explain why the subject of nihilism is an important one and why it should be at the heart of our concerns. This issue is very much neglected, and it should be getting our careful attention. Upon establishing the importance of the issue, I will elaborate on its relation to "higher values", which are typically upheld by a society. Through this, I hope to give the reader a clearer understanding of the issues at hand and a framework with which to better follow the discussion throughout the rest of the book.

Furthermore, once I have shown that the possibility of nihilism opens through the collapse of certain collectively held higher values, I will be able to transition into giving a particular example of when nihilistic deterioration occurs with specific attention given to the concept of truth. I intend to outline how valuing truth in a particular way can lead to undermining the value for truth completely, and therefore lead a society into what is referred to as a "post-truth era". I hope to demonstrate how the transition from the former era to the latter allows for conditions to arise which lead to a societal mental exhaustion, which in turn leads to an increase in forms of escapism to avoid having to face "the burden of consciousness". That is, the burden of having to face up to the difficulties of life, the suffering it entails, the task of figuring out what it means to live, what is going on in the world, and where you fit into all of this exactly. I will explore how these forms of escapism are overabundant in our society, how it overwhelms us, and therefore, how we become mentally paralysed and incapable of making any genuine internal progress.

Nihilism is an individual sickness as well as a collective disease, that we are all having to face either directly or indirectly. These threats to meaning are present whether we like to think so or not. Turning a blind eye to the conditions that I will be outlining does not make them go away, nor does it resolve the issue; it only makes it worse. We must face it head on by first recognising its existence. Only then can we attempt to overcome it. This sickness will be diagnosed, and an antidote prescribed.

The symptoms of this sickness will be assessed and outlined, looking first at the effects of nihilism on ideas and thinking. Technology and scientific advancement are often praised as a way in which we will transcend many of these issues. However, I wish to show that counter to this opinion, technological advancements, rather than being something to praise, can be seen as facilitating this escapism through what is termed "Techno-Hypnosis".

I will then move on to look at the effects of nihilism on people and society. I will identify issues arising out of the lack of a collective societal aims or goals, and how this increases the societal fracturing we are currently experiencing throughout the world. All these problems have a necessary effect on how we think about many areas of life, including politics, morality, moral duty, and meaning. I intend to explore and highlight all of this in an approachable way for the average person to be able to digest and understand.

I will ascertain how many people try to flee nihilism by picking and choosing elements from many different religions they find useful, while paradoxically rejecting religion as "backwards" or "dogmatic". That is, I wish to show how the nihilist (whether they know themselves to be one or not), as much as they push religion away, do not actually escape religiosity. They try to belittle such concepts as "faith" yet are caught repeatedly making numerous leaps of faith themselves.

From here we will move to the latter part of the book which has two aims. Firstly, to remove common obstacles that might get in the way of someone taking religion seriously, and secondly, going over exactly how Islam acts as a solution to the causes of nihilism and the cure to its effects.

With regards to the obstacles, we will discuss the question on whether we should be believing in the divine, what the evidence is exactly, how to overcome the problem of multiple gods/religions, the essence of traditions, and the concept of faith and its inevitability. I will also ask the reader to take a leap of faith with me, but I will not give too much about that right now.

When discussing how Islam deals with the causes and the effects of nihilism, we will go through each of the things we have raised in earlier parts of the book, and referring to Islamic scripture to show how these two positions are incompatible, and that if you embrace Islam and believes in it, you can expect to resolve these issues completely.

PART ONE

Beginning to Understand Nihilism

The Philosophy of Nihilism

The human being is driven by many needs such as sustenance, shelter, and community, but we are also heavily driven by purpose. Insofar as nihilism is the explicit denial that life has any purpose, it is necessarily so that nihilism denies our humanity. This has the danger of expressing itself in a variety of ways, and so to avoid its consequences we need to work hard at understanding it intimately.

Nihilism can come in many forms, but generally speaking, it can be described as the rejection of all meaning, purpose, and the disintegration of traditional morality.[1] David Matheson defines nihilism as maintaining that "no lives are, all things considered, worth living";[2] and Raff Donelson further describes a particular form of nihilism as holding that "life is somehow meaningless, hollow" and again, "not worth living".[3] As we can see from these descriptions, nihilism is not an optimistic worldview, but a pessimistic one.

Friedrich Nietzsche, who is considered the father of the philosophy of nihilism, adds to this concept by saying that "there is no goal, no answer to the question: why?"; and further builds on this by saying, "what is the significance of nihilism? – that the highest values devalue themselves."[4] The feature of "not having a goal", and of the "highest values devalue[ing] themselves" will be one of the central subjects of the first part of this book.

Before I continue with this however, it is important to understand why nihilism should be of interest, not just to me (as is hopefully clear after reading the preface), but also to you.

---

1   Britannica, The Editors of Encyclopaedia. 'Nihilism'. *Encyclopedia Britannica*, 13 March 2020
2   Matheson D., 'Incoherence of Soft Nihilism', *Think*, 47/16, (2017) 127-135 (p.127)
3   Donelson R, 'The Nihilist', *The Pragmatism and Prejudice of Oliver Wendell Holmes Jr.*, Edited by Vannatta S., (Maryland: Lexington Books, 2019) p. 3
4   Nietzsche F., *The Will to Power*, (London: Penguin Group, 2017) p. 15

The Importance of Nihilism

It is crucial that we clarify exactly why it is we should care. Why should we spend our time looking into it at all? The reason I say that your concern is necessary is that the feeling of nihilism will very possibly strike you at some point in life if it has not already. However, if you are blessed enough to never be affected by it, the chances are that at the very least somebody you know, and love, will. Alternatively, you may not know that you have been affected by it because the word "nihilism" is a strange one that you may not be familiar with; it is not often heard by the average person or brought up in day-to-day conversation. It may very well be the case that upon reading this book you come to realise that you have in fact experienced nihilism, but you just did not know there was a philosophical term for it. In any case, I wish to convince you that it is important, and that it does require *our* attention, not just mine alone. I wish to convince you that if we fail in this regard, people's lives (and potentially their afterlife) are at stake.

The philosopher Albert Camus, in his book *The Myth of Sisyphus*, opens his book by saying "[t]here is but one truly serious philosophical problem and that is suicide."[5] The philosopher Arthur Schopenhauer, who was well known for his pessimism, made some anti-natalist[6] remarks which follow this "anti-life" theme, which is the notion that life is just not worth beginning, never mind living. Although this certainly is not to say that he is promoting suicide as an answer, he does state quite clearly that we should not even bother bringing life into existence:

> "If children were brought into the world by an act of pure reason alone, would the human race continue to exist? Would not a man rather have so much sympathy with the coming generation as to spare it the burden of existence? Or at any rate not take it upon

---
5   Camus A., *The Myth of Sisyphus*, (London: Penguin Books, 2005), p 1.
6   The belief that life is not worth beginning and that having children is immoral.

himself to impose that burden upon it in cold blood."[7]

Schopenhauer's work was a massive influence on Nietzsche, and it was most definitely a contributing factor to the work he produced on pessimism and nihilism. However, we cannot lay the development of these ideas only at the feet of these two philosophers. You could argue that it is the many philosophical ideas themselves that have been littering the field of philosophy which have slowly evolved into nihilism; therefore, giving rise to this anti-life sentiment (expressed through either anti-natalist, suicidal, or both). This theme has built momentum over the years, and you see its fruition in the sheer numbers of people that are ending their lives today. The World Health Organisation released an article stating that close to 800,000 people end their lives worldwide *every year*; and for every successful suicide there are many more failed attempts.[8] To put this into perspective, this is like finding out that every year a city the size of Leeds, in the UK, has ended their own lives, and a number of other cities of a similar size (2 to 4 of them) have attempted to do so but failed. This is a clear sign of the prevalence of severe unhappiness, and that life is considered not worth living for a very large number of people. On top of this you also have people who consider it, desire it, but do not attempt to end their lives, possibly out of fear of it going wrong or being painful. But in any case, they still consider life not worth living to warrant desiring to take such drastic action at all. Furthermore, data quality and collection methods are lacking in many countries around the world, so these figures might in fact be much worse than the data we have at present suggests. Nonetheless, the figures as they stand are still very high and this is concerning. Lastly, the connection between this problem of suicide and depression and the issue of nihilism is the idea that life is either meaningless, without purpose, or not worth living at all.

In Martin Heidegger's book *Being and Time,* he outlines the idea that what makes *Dasein* [roughly speaking, the human being], distinct from other beings is that its very existence is an issue for it.[9] That is, unlike other beings, the human being must decide what *kind* of a being it is going to be. The human being must decide *how to be*. Will this person decide to work towards being an engineer, an artist, a lawyer, a doctor, or a philosopher? It must project itself into the future, set goals, and work towards attaining these

---

7   Schopenhauer A., *The Essays of Arthur Schopenhauer: Studies in Pessimism,* Vol. 4, Trans. By T. Bailey Saunders, (Pennsylvania: The Pennsylvania State University, 2005), p.7
8   World Health Organisation (WHO), 'Suicide', *WHO*, 2 Sept. 2019,
9   Heidegger M., *Being & Time,* (Oxford: Blackwell Publishing LTD, 2016), page 68.

goals. The human being drags the ideal out from the realm of mind and into the world, into reality. Other beings do not have to concern themselves with such things. The lion, the bird, the fish, and the insect do not need to figure out how to be, they just *are what they are,* and they just *do what they do.* There is very little room or reason for an existential crisis.[10] The human being on the other hand could have everything they desire and have attained all earthly needs and wants in abundance, yet still become depressed and suicidal. The human being cannot help but ponder over the meaning of life. We strive for purpose not for the sake of it, but because it is an integral part of our very being! This is why the issue of nihilism is important, and this is why we should be concerned with it.

---

10 Existential crisis being the felt experience of not understanding the purpose behind your life, and yet having an overwhelming desire to have or obtain an understanding. It can also include the experience that such an understanding is beyond your ability to grasp.

Nihilism's Relevance to Goals and Values

Let me begin by explaining what a value is, and then by giving an example that explains how the highest values undermine themselves, as this is often a source of confusion for those first hearing it. When talking about "value", what is meant is something which is considered of relative worth, utility, or importance.[11] We can talk of material things having value, but we can also talk of ideas or principles having it too. When talking about higher values, what I am referring to are the principles or standards which individuals or collectives hold as the most important.

So important in fact that they feel they have a duty to maintain or uphold these for themselves and their society. They are what a community considers as *the* most important things, and can be what unites them as a people, or what they collectively consider to be of great worth and utility. Religion is a great example of this; in the Muslim world, Islam, that is, the worship of and submission to God, is *the* highest value. To an Atheist, maybe Secularism or personal Liberty is the thing that should be valued the most. These higher values can be expressed in a multitude of ways depending on the people and context. You can visualise it as a pyramid, with the most important things/ideas being at the top, and the least important at the bottom.

---

11   Merriam-Webster, 'Value', *Merriam-Webster Dictionary*,

A Higher Value Undermining Itself

You may find an example of a higher value undermining itself within the "Christian West" concerning the idea of truth.[12] Truth was made a higher value to the point that it began to undermine the very foundations that gave rise to the value in the first place. But how did it become a higher value? Prior to Christianity, Europe was mostly polytheistic in its worship, dedicating themselves to multiple gods. Now although there certainly were instances of the gods acting truthfully, there were also examples of them acting in very questionable ways. The Greek god Zeus, for example, is notorious for raping women. There are also numerous examples of lying by both the ancient gods and heroes of the past.[13] There was such an emphasis on cheating, lying and deception in ancient polytheistic religions that Socrates himself, in Plato's *Republic*, had to discuss censoring them for this very reason. In the preliminary writing to the chapter, the following was stated as a commentary by the editor on what was to follow in Plato's dialogue:

> "It must also be remembered that the Greeks had no Bible, and what the Bible has been to us as a source of theology and morals, poets were to the Greeks. And if Plato seems very preoccupied with the morals and theological aspect of the poets it is because it was from them the ordinary Greek was expected to acquire his moral and theological notions."[14]

---

12   By Christian West, I recognise that the West is not so much Christian anymore, but rather secular. The use of the term Christian in this regard, is to highlight the origins, history, and foundation of the particular people we will be discussing here. I also recognise that "the west", is not so much a description of a geographical direction, but rather of the remains of the empire that "the west" had created during its expansionist efforts in the early modern period. For example, Australia would be included with the term "west", despite it being in the east.
13   Shilling A., 'Famous Liars in Greek Mythology', *Classroom synonym*,
14   Plato, *The Republic*, Trans. By D. Lee, (London: Penguin Books, 2007), p. 67.

This issue was notably something the ancients had to deal with, as pantheons of gods in ancient religions always contained a plethora of different characters, many of whom were at odds with each other. Socrates despised these stories so much, due to their nature, and the problems that I have alluded to here, that he said:

> "And they shall not be repeated in our state, Adeimantus, nor shall any young audience be told that anyone who commits horrible crimes, or punishes his father unmercifully, is doing nothing out of the ordinary but merely what the first and greatest of the gods have done before."[15]

Socrates is one of the most well-known and well-respected western philosophers in history,[16] and he was quick to point this problem out. Now with the rise of Christianity, a solution to this problem became present in the Bible. Lying became "an abomination to The Lord"; on the other hand, "those who act faithfully are His delight".[17] In another part the believer is commanded to become "a worker who has no need to be ashamed, rightly handling the word of truth."[18]

Truth became a central emphasis of the doctrine, and followers were warned of severe punishment for going astray. Unlike the previous religions, where the many gods acting in abhorrent ways opened the potential for this to be justified, Christianity warned that "a false witness will not go unpunished, and he who breathes out lies will perish."[19] Truthfulness became present as an explicit command by *the* highest value – God. Because of this, His commands were necessarily to be valued above everything else as well.

However, with what Nietzsche referred to as the "death of God" (the loss of faith) in the western world, motivation for this moral underpinning was also lost. With that, their justification, and their foundation to the ability to claim that something was good *absolutely* was taken away from them. Their valuing of truth became "free floating", as it were, and it was assumed to be "self-evident". However, philosophy is known for leaving nothing unquestioned; it explores everything and leaves no stone unturned. Eventually, the false assumption that truth is a *necessary* higher value in a secular/atheistic world, held independently from the commands of God

---

15   ibid, p.70
16   For more on Socrates, read here: Kraut, R. "Socrates". *Encyclopedia Britannica*, 23 Dec. 2020,
17   The Holy Bible, English Standard Version, Proverbs 12:22,
18   ibid, 2 Timothy 2:15
19   ibid, Proverbs 19:9

(who they no longer had faith in), began to crumble. This becomes especially evident when people became more focused on worldly things and began to be more concerned with philosophical ideas like utilitarianism.[20]

When values are being rooted in sensations like pleasure and pain, this becomes a paradigm through which truth itself can potentially be seen as an evil, *necessarily*. If truth ever happens to get in the way of the greatest amount of pleasure for the greatest amount of people, what motivation remains to value truth? If it happens to be the case that a grand lie is best suited for providing such an end, truth can very quickly be abandoned for something more satisfying. However, this is not something that would occur overnight. Christianity has been around for so long that its moral system has become somewhat ingrained into the very foundations of western society, and many of its moral axioms are taken for granted.

---

[20]   In short, the idea that good can be reduced to that which causes the most pleasure for the greatest number of people and minimises suffering.

PART 2

The Causes & Effects of Nihilism

The Rise of "Post-Truth"

It is this historical movement that I have just been describing in the previous section, especially from the beginning of the enlightenment period through to the widespread loss of faith, which can be said to have led to what is now described as the "post-truth" era. Expressing concern, the Guardian newspaper writes: "In our new normal, experts are dismissed, and alternative facts flagrantly offered. This suspicion of specialists is part of a bigger problem."[21] We have entered a strange period where the commitment to truth, inherited from Christian roots, has revealed a seemingly unavoidable scepticism which spawns out of the issues surrounding the nature of having to trust "the experts".

Trust is a central feature of any society. The average citizen does not have the time or the ability to understand the (often very esoteric) nature of the fields that expert's study in great depth and for long periods of time. They must therefore have faith in them for any relationship between the two parties to function productively. That is, of course, so long as these experts are in fact trustworthy. This relationship always leaves open the possibility of trust being abused via manipulation and corruption, as the laymen do not have the knowledge or the ability to recognise when this trust has been violated to call it out. This is an ever-present threat in all societies.

The issues surrounding corruption and dishonesty have become more apparent because of direct access to sources of information like the internet. Organisations such as *Wikileaks* (and others) have released a plethora of information exposing the corruption that is commonplace within governments and corporations alike. Such revelations have had a huge impact on the overall trust in the US government for example, with the percentage of people who trust them dropping from nearly 80% in the 1960's to less than 20% in the present day.[22] If one scandal after another is constantly

---

21   Enfield N., "We're in a post-truth world with eroding trust and accountability." *The Guardian Newspaper*, 16 November 2017,
22   Pew Research Centre, "Public Trust in Government: 1958-2019", *Pew Research*

being uncovered and publicised all over the internet, it is understandable that this would have major effects on the levels of trust.

Centre, 11 April 2019,

Societal Exhaustion

It is understandable, with the conditions that I have outlined thus far in place, that this could lead to the rise of what I will call a *societal exhaustion*. That is, the collective mental fatigue and confusion brought about by there being too many varying opinions on too many subjects expressed by too many "experts". This makes many people feel incapable of finding the truth, and so in large numbers give up on being able to attain it at all or they fall into some form of relativism. Hence the popularisation of phrases like "my truth", indicating that truth is somehow necessarily subjective.

A lot of the ideas that many people in society have taken for granted for centuries have now been put into question. In academia, all of that which was previously taken for granted has been dissected and analysed. The discussion for the justification or dismissal of such ideas has become increasingly complex and esoteric. Furthermore, when these discussions take place in the public sphere it often becomes heated and controversial. As if the mental energy required to cover such topics was not demanding enough, throwing anxiety into the mix certainly does not help matters improve. This is especially the case for those who have jobs to hold, families to spend time with, and rest to catch up on. All while having very little time to cover these "hot topics" extensively enough to grasp them sufficiently. These subjects can be difficult for dedicated academics, let alone the public. How can they be expected to absorb all of this during a fiery discussion on evening television after a long hard day at work. The issue here is further amplified when those on either side of the debate are trying to get the intended audience to incline towards the position they are propagating, and not for a position of admitting your own inability to comprehend the problems at hand, in the little time you have been given to explore it. Therefore, if the public does incline to one position or the other, they are not doing so out of having knowledge, but rather, out of being persuaded via the most appealing rhetoric. Truth under these conditions becomes democratic in a problematic way, because the populous is being led to hold opinions, not knowledge, about subjects they know nearly nothing about.

All of this is coupled with the fact that we have *all* been overwhelmed by the mass of information available on the internet. This relatively new resource is so large that it is beyond the capacity of the collaborative efforts of everyone on the planet to be able to process comprehensively. This inability to process the information would necessarily make establishing what the truth is, even more difficult. Furthermore, we may know more now than we have ever known in the past about the natural world, but every answer has brought with it many more questions. Paradoxically, we now know that we *do not know* much more than we have ever previously been able to imagine. In the pursuit of truth, instead of making life and the world more intelligible or clear, there are very good grounds for the argument that this pursuit has only made it even more confusing and harder to grasp; intensifying its mystery, complexity, and leaving the average person less sure about themselves and their place in the universe (whatever these things are). Hence why it can be said that the higher value (truth), has undermined itself. The pursuit of truth has led to an overabundance of information that we are completely incapable of processing sufficiently enough to be able to say we have any idea of what's going on.

Overwhelmed by Overabundance

I will now explore how this overabundance can motivate the onset of nihilism. In the 1970's, the author Alvin Toffler mentioned some of the predictions people had made about the trajectory of the future. He points to the thought of a few individuals who saw the rise of an increasingly standardised culture, and makes special mention of the thought of Jacques Ellul:

> According to Ellul, man was far freer in the past when "Choice was a real possibility for him." By contrast, today, "The human being is no longer in any sense the agent of choice." And, as for tomorrow: "In the future, man will apparently be confined to the role of a recording device." Robbed of choice, he will be acted upon, not active. He will live, Ellul warns, in a totalitarian state run by a velvet-gloved Gestapo.[23]

Now although I can be sure that many people would still think Ellul was on to something here, I think Toffler had a very good counter argument. Contrary to Ellul, Toffler thought the issue for the future had less to do with the absence of choices, but rather the overabundance of choices, to the extent that it causes paralysis. He says that "[t]hey may turn out to be victims of that peculiarly super-industrial dilemma: overchoice."[24]

Furthermore, he goes on to explain this concept by adding that it gives rise to "the point at which the advantages of diversity and individualization are cancelled by the complexity of the buyer's decision-making process."[25] He happily admits that diversity and individualization may very well have its advantages, people may feel a sense of uniqueness about themselves which helps to make the choices feel special. However, if the complexity of the choice becomes too much, the amount of stress this causes might

---

23 Toffler A., *Future Shock* (New York: Random House Inc., 1971) p. 263
24 ibid.,
25 ibid.,

completely nullify any positive feelings that may have had the chance to arise. Here he is specifically talking about purchasing items, but this can just as easily be applied to ideas or subject matters for research. To learn about something, you must first choose which path of learning you wish to take. However, to do that you must first sift through the available options which are unquantifiable.

We see this issue express itself very often within the atheistic/agnostic apologetics circles, when they reject all religions based on the sheer number of them (which I will also talk more about later in this book). It is this which will help to highlight the absurdity behind the naive belief that more freedom, and more choices to exercise that freedom with, is necessarily a good thing. To the contrary, it can in fact cause paralysis and the inability to make a choice altogether out of fear of picking the wrong one. Furthermore, it can also cause dissatisfaction and motivate the inability to enjoy whatever was chosen, simply because of the ever-present possibility of having not made the best possible choice. Yes, this flavour ice cream is nice, but what if that other one was better?

I want to make something clear. It is very well the case that a limited choice can be better than no choice at all, in a good number of circumstances. I do not deny this. However, it certainly does not follow from this that endless choices are necessarily better than a limited amount of choice. The psychologist Barry Schwartz goes on to confirm Toffler's predictions in his book *The Paradox of Choice*.[26] In his TedTalk's presentation, inspired by his book, he outlines the '*official dogma*' as follows, and I paraphrase:

> "The aim is to maximise welfare, which means to maximise freedom and choice. More freedom means there will be more choices, and more choices means there will be greater welfare."[27]

He claims this assumption is false and lists a few reasons why too much choice makes people miserable. Firstly, they can suffer from regret and/or anticipated regret, as I've already mentioned. You make a choice, but the other one could have been better. Secondly, due to the costs of opportunity on things, such as time and resources which cannot always be retrieved again (especially with time). Thirdly, due to an inflation of expectations that is caused by the increase of choice. If you manage to pick something which you think is the best choice, you or others may have hyped it up

---

26   Schwartz B., The Paradox of Choice: Why More Is Less, (New York: HarperCollins Publishers Inc., 2016)
27   Nagel T., 'The Absurd', *The Journal of Philosophy*, 68/20, (1971), 716-727, (p. 718)

so much that it doesn't meet the experience that you were expecting. Last of all, self-blame. If it is *you* that has made the wrong choice, who else is there to blame but yourself? How silly were you for not making a better choice! "Oh, woe is me."

Now as I've already briefly mentioned, if we take into consideration the huge number of religions there are, political decisions that need to be made, ethical theories you can subscribe to, or all the other things that the modern person is faced with choosing from, it is not difficult to see why choosing not to choose might seem very attractive (even if somewhat paradoxical). It is simply less effort. Furthermore, linking this back to Nietzsche, we now have the foundation from which this pathological state of nihilism might arise. This choice paralysis described by Toffler and Schwartz maps on very well to the characteristics of the psychological exhaustion the average person might experience in the face of "information overload". This, in turn, can give rise to the feeling of "the absurd" that many of the existential philosophers were famous for discussing. For Albert Camus, this was the utter failure of the world to meet our expectations, or the result of the ideals that we have in our minds not successfully mapping onto reality. For Thomas Nagel it was better described as the conflict between the seriousness with which we took our lives, and the ever-present possibility of considering all of which we take seriously as "arbitrary or open for doubt."[28]

---

28 Nagel T., 'The Absurd', *The Journal of Philosophy*, 68/20, (1971), 716-727, (p. 718)

Nihilism as a Sickness

So far, I have discussed several important issues. First, I discussed what is meant by the term "nihilism", and how higher values relate to this. I have also delved into concepts such as higher values, post-truth, and societal exhaustion. I now wish to transition into a discussion on how the nihilistic state of being should be understood. That is, it should be seen as a sickness of meaninglessness and pervasive insignificance. Having understood some of the causes and developments of this sickness, and by explaining this diagnosis a little more in this section, I will explore further in the following sections its effects. First, by looking at the effects of this sickness on ideas and thinking, and then its effects on people and society.

Nietzsche referred to nihilism as "an intermediary pathological state."[29] This portrays the condition more as a temporary mental disorder that you must overcome, rather than as a philosophical choice made after careful deliberation. It is not characterised by a fully informed rational exploration, but by an exhaustion and the "immense generalisation, the inference *that life has no meaning whatsoever*."[30] So, it is not necessarily the result of logical and valid deduction but of a hasty generalisation.

Most people that experience life as meaningless have not gone through the process of writing it down analytically to work out if they have a valid argument with true premises. Rather, it arises as an experience, as something felt. Many of these people have likely not been trained in the field of logic and reasoning, and so it would be unreasonable to expect many people to be so rigid with such things. This is not to disparage the average person, nor how they approach things. I think it would be unfair (and rather elitist) to expect everyone to act like academic philosophers, and to do so intuitively and without the training. Life is hard and it can beat down the best of us. No amount of rigorous training in university can equip you to overcome every issue.

---

29 Nietzsche F., *The Will to Power*, (UK: Penguin Books, 2017), p. 20.
30 Ibid.

Not only that, if the person in question here is not well inclined to such tasks, making them go through such a process might only worsen their condition rather than to alleviate it. If someone is struggling with a sense of meaninglessness and helplessness, throwing too much philosophical jargon around is not going to be the best course of action for them. We must endeavour to navigate this carefully and be empathetic to the individuals we have to deal with and be sure to carve out a clear path to higher ground where careful deliberation can take place.

The onset of nihilism is induced. It is a pathological state caused by mental exhaustion, but it is still something that *can* be overcome; not something we should aim to exasperate. Nietzsche himself saw nihilism as something that needed to be overcome, and not a state you should remain in. Nature abhors a vacuum as they say. But we must ask the question: Is there anything else that causes the feelings of the meaninglessness of life to arise?

The author Philip Phenix, in his book "Realms of Meaning", points out several factors which are a threat to the experience of meaning and significance. He says the "perennial threat to meaning is intensified under the conditions of modern industrial civilisation",[31] and goes on to list four factors which lead to this intensification. That is:

1. The spirit of criticism and scepticism which dominate the domains of science and philosophy, among many other fields.

2. The tendency towards depersonalisation and the fragmenting of complex societies due to industrialisation and alienation.

3. Overabundance of both things and information, inevitably overwhelming the modern citizen.

4. Rapid rates of change which leave a constant feeling of impermanence and lack of security.[32]

According to Phenix, all these factors combined contribute to an overall increased sense of meaninglessness, and the experience of a lack of significance. Unfortunately, all of this can potentially further contribute to rates of suicide, depression, and substance abuse in a society.[33] This would no doubt likely further contribute to the sense of nihilism that prevails

---

31   Phenix P. H., *Realms of Meaning*, (New York: McGraw-Hill Book Company, 1964), p.5.
32   Ibid.
33   Heisel, M.J. & Flett, G.L., "Purpose in Life, Satisfaction with Life, and Suicide Ideation in a Clinical Sample", *Journal of Psychopathology and Behavioural Assessment*, 26/127, (2004)

over all those affected by the increase of such things happening around them; a nasty feedback loop to say the least. You might also notice that the four factors listed here are much more prevalent today than they were in the 1960's when Phenix published his book. Although they were still very relevant then, the conditions he has outlined have only intensified as time progressed.

Truth & Techno-Hypnosis

It was naively thought that the pursuit for as much truth as possible would certainly be a benefit for society. However, it seems mainly to have led to a thirst for advances in technology which make life more convenient and increases our leisure opportunities, without ever asking if this should necessarily be considered a benefit nor consider its potentially negative effects. One such type of consequence is the *techno-hypnosis* offered through technological escapism as outlined in the work of the author Nolen Gertz, in his book *Nihilism & Technology*.[34] This idea is linked to what Nietzsche refers to as "self-hypnosis", wherein the human being turns to technology to zone out from reality. That is, to be completely distracted to avoid life and being human.

 Many people appear to have developed a desire to avoid the burden of consciousness and having to think too deeply about the big questions on life and existence. Instead, we turn to things like Netflix, YouTube, or social media to facilitate a self-inflicted hypnosis. The task of trying to figure out exactly what is going on is daunting and has no end in sight. Engaging in petty tasks which distract us from such burdens is a very effective way of avoiding having to give focus to the burdens of consciousness altogether. You need only to look at what pop culture is currently pouring out to meet the demands of the public desire to zone out and forget about their problems: reality TV shows, prank YouTube channels, the gaming industry, etc. All of this [and more] offers a great deal of mind-numbing entertainment for the needs of the modern populous. We mined the world for information and have amassed more than we ever thought possible, yet the average person is still more enamoured by illusion and fantasy. They appear to be more ready and eager to escape reality, not immerse themselves in it. We set out in search of truth and became overwhelmed and confused by it, so now the average person seeks comfort elsewhere by hiding from it. Like

---

[34] Gertz N., *Nihilism and Technology*, (London: Rowman & Littlefield International LTD, 2018), pp. 60-63.

those who are mentioned in Plato's cave analogy, who hate the one that tries to remove them from their chains.[35]

The issue here is that this technological escapism hardly offers the individuals who engage in it the opportunity to feel any significance or any genuine sense of meaning in their lives. As mentioned at the beginning of this book, it is heart breaking that one of the leading causes of death in young people is suicide. On average someone ends their life once every 40 seconds; and for every person that has successfully killed themselves, there are even more who have attempted suicide.[36] Alongside this, rates of depression and anxiety are on the increase, and it is said that "[p]arallel lines of evidence indicate that modernization is generally associated with higher rates of depression."[37] So we have more truths than ever before, and we have now obtained truths about how the industrialised collection of these truths has led to conditions which increase the general standards of living, yet at the same time also (paradoxically) leads to increases in suicide and the deteriorating mental health. Thus, increasing a reliance on effective means of escaping having to face our mortality and problems by immersing ourselves in braindead technological escapism. This again gives rise to further questions: If we are so busy trying to escape the burden of consciousness via technology, does this have any effect on our sense of duty to society? Does this escapism not also mean to escape our community? Is society, and the people that make it up, not necessarily a part of the reality we are avoiding?

---

[35] "And if anyone tried to release them and lead them up, they would kill him if they could lay hands on him." - Plato, *The Republic*, Trans. By D. Lee, (London: Penguin Books, 2007), p. 243.

[36] World Health Organisation, 'Mental Health and Substance Use', WHO,

[37] Hidaka B. H., 'Depression as a Disease of Modernity: Explanations for Increasing Prevalence.', *Journal of Affective Disorders*, 140/3 (2012),

Society, Obligation & Duty

It follows that if we see the world as something that we need to escape, we are necessarily escaping the people that populate that world, as the two are intimately connected. The German philosopher Martin Heidegger, in his work *Being & Time*, describes the human as a being that is a "Being-in-the-world".[38] That is, we do not simply exist in the world like a *thing*, or an *object* exists in it. The way you or I exist in the world is not equivalent to the way chocolates exist in a box. To describe the human being in such a way completely misses something fundamental that makes the human distinct. Describing this, William Large says:

> To think of our world in this way would be to confuse our way of Being with the Being of things, which is precisely what we should not do. I do not exist in the same way as the glass does. There is no doubt that I can be treated that way. In a certain way of looking at things, I too can appear as a thing. Seen in a photograph, I might seem to a casual observer to be merely in a room in the same way that water is in a glass. Even here, it is possible to look at the picture in a different way. The expression of my face might tell you how I felt at the time. Perhaps I look miserable or uncomfortable. Perhaps my world was not quite right with me. The expression 'my world', and the fact you understand it in a certain way, already tells you there is quite a difference between me and the water in the glass. In what sense can we say the water has its own world? Yet it is very easy for us to think about ourselves and others in this way. What else am I asking about when I meet

---

38   Heidegger calls this *"Dasein"* - A German word that translates to "there-being", which Heidegger used to express the kind of being the human is. It is an ontological description that is meant to explain the way we are, rather than simply what we are. That is, the description is not meant to be an ontic one.

you in the street and say, "How are you?" Am I not asking about your world?[39]

We recognise this of ourselves, fundamentally, and of others. The very nature of our being demands we recognise this fact. We have our worlds, our perspectives, our unique subjectivities. A further thing that Heidegger recognises in his work is that attached to this notion of "Being-in-the-World" is also the idea that we are a "Being-with-Others". That is, we have an inescapable relation to the way we are in the world with other people, and "it is a part of what it means to be me".[40] I cannot escape the Other. Even when alone, we are only alone in so far as we recognise the Other is absent.

Now if the human being is trying to escape the burden of consciousness by escaping the world into artificial forms of entertainment, then they are necessarily escaping their relation to other human beings which are intimately tied to our experience of the world. You may argue in retort to this that there are still others present in this escape, be that the actors in films, or characters in games. However, the important difference here is any relation with such others is artificial and one way. They may impact us, and we may see them and hear them, but it does not occur the other way around.

In this escape from the world, and inevitably the escape from others, you are potentially removing any sense of duty towards the community as well. With the rise of convenience technology there is a rise in the physical isolation of people. Cars isolate us from each other on our journeys and leave us stuck in our own little bubbles. Public transport is filled with people glued to their mobile devices with earphones in, occupying our sight and hearing and letting the other fade away into the background. There is a decrease in communal religious gatherings in the West,[41] which are rapidly being replaced with weekend binges fuelled by alcohol and drugs. In the UK alone, there are over half a million dependent drinkers,[42] and in a survey reported by the Independent, 68% of those questioned described their neighbours as "strangers" and 73% said they did not know their neighbour's names.[43] People don't know the names of the people who live next door,

---

39   Large W., *Heidegger's Being and Time*, (Edinburgh: Edinburgh University Press, 2008), p. 34.
40   ibid, p. 118.
41   Pew Research Center, 'In U.S., Decline of Christianity Continues at Rapid Pace', *Pew Research Center*, 17 October 2019,
42   Alcohol Change UK, 'Alcohol Statistics', *Alcohol Change UK*,
43   Elsworthy E., 'More than half of Britons describe their neighbours as 'strangers'', *Independent*, 29 May 2018,

but they know the names of the celebrities that populate their shows, and probably know more about their lives than people who live close enough to hear you scream for help were you ever in trouble. This is a huge problem, but a very telling one with regards to our relationship to technology, and our sense of duty to those around us.

Earlier on, I made a particular focus on truth as a higher value to show that societies must orient themselves according to the things that they value the most. That may be truth, but it could also be the good of the community, pleasure, freedom, reason, security, etc.[44] Once the values have been established, the society must then move towards the goals that help achieve the manifestation of those values. These concepts and ideas become the foundation for everything that begins to develop out of these communities. However, they are ultimately underpinned by the belief that such values are a *moral duty* upon the individuals that make up the community, and it is that which binds them together as a collective. For truth to be a higher value, it must first be seen as good! That is, it must be something desired, and considered to be beneficial in one way or another. However, if at any point truth is shown to be detrimental, what motivation remains to hold truth with such high regard? What moral duty binds the people to truth when it ceases to benefit them?

From the perspective of a society that has lost faith in their foundational traditions, and who have removed God from their social sphere, the motivating factors that necessarily commit people to truth— such as fear of eternal punishment— are no longer present. The same can be said with regards to the fear of punishment for the sin of committing suicide. In a secular world, the loss of God in the hearts of people can be accompanied by a rise in doubts and scepticism. This also opens the door to thoughts of what one is potentially missing out on. If there is no afterlife, no ultimate accountability, why should someone necessarily care about justice, truth, or the community at large? Especially if these things require great sacrifice from the individual that get in the way of experiencing intense pleasure and doing what you really want to do.

Take the words of the popular YouTube channel *Kurzgesagt* for example, where in a video on the subject of "Optimistic Nihilism" they say:

> "You only get one shot at life, which is scary, but it also sets you free. If the universe ends in heat death, every humiliation you suffer in your life will be forgotten. *Every mistake you made will not matter in the end. Every bad thing you did will be voided. If*

---

44   It should also be noted here that some of these values can come into conflict with one another. For example, freedom and security.

our life is all we get to experience, then it's the only thing that matters. If the universe has no principles, the only principles relevant are the ones we decide on."[45] [Emphasis mine]

The above quote was taken from a video that has so far received over 16 million views and over 900 thousand likes, along with tens of thousands of comments of praise. It can hardly be said to be an insignificant movement that is not worthy of attention. Nihilism has clearly taken a hold of popular consciousness and videos such as the one I have referenced are attempts to combat this reality.

However, I would like to draw attention to the fact that the quote itself expresses some troubling remarks. These remarks have inferences that help us to better understand the core of this philosophy. If every mistake you make will not matter, then why worry about making mistakes? If every bad thing you did will be voided, then why not do bad things? What does bad even mean? Does it even exist? If our life is the only thing that matters, then why should anyone (necessarily) care about the lives of other people?

Recently there was a video going viral on social media of a man who covered a kitten in fuel and set it on fire, only to watch (and record) it run around in the dark hopelessly until it burned to death. If the perpetrator of this heinous crime was to watch Kurzgesagt's video, would it help convince him that he should feel guilt or remorse for what he did? Or rather, would it only increase his sense of security that in the end every bad thing he did "will be voided" and that he has nothing to worry about? After all, this optimistic nihilism has "set him free". I do not think Kurzgesagt had such people in mind when making this video, but nonetheless, such viewers are certainly going to find them relieving, if not comforting. And these kinds of viewers most certainly exist. Every year globally there are around 400,000 homicides: that's a lot of murderers. Not to mention the psychopaths that simply hurt others without killing them.

Furthermore, commitment to truth for such individuals would not necessarily be beneficial at all. If truth is an obstacle for benefit or gain, or it was to take away their freedom, then why would they necessarily feel the need to care about the truth? The attachment to truth in such cases would quickly become pragmatic and dropped if it was not useful to hold on to it. That is, it would be accepted on the basis that it works towards a certain end. It is important to note and emphasise here that I am in no way claiming that everyone who is secular or nihilistic (knowingly or unknowingly) would necessarily become psychopaths like the gentleman

---

45 Kurzgesagt – In a Nutshell, "Optimistic Nihilism", 26 July 2017, (timestamp: 3 minutes 45 seconds)

I have mentioned above. This is clearly an absurd conclusion. The point of mentioning this is simply to outline that the creators of this video have taken a very naive and idealistic approach to nihilism and towards their perception of their audience. They have clearly not considered the potential implications of this thought process and have failed to justify why anyone should necessarily be empathetic towards others at all. What they have espoused is fertile grounds for a selfish philosophy, or other systems of thought centred around the will to power.

A Fractured Society

The emphasis on valuing freedom and individuality in the Western world has led to portions of the society moving in very different directions on several different subjects. As an example, a study by pew research has shown that from 1994 to 2014, the US has become more divided as time has moved forward. There is significantly less political overlap or common agreement between different parties now, than there was over 20 years ago.[46] A people can only move forward together, towards something collectively, if they can agree on what to aim at and how to achieve it. Historically, that collective aim would be encapsulated by the tradition. Now, however, with an emphasis on the rejection of tradition and a focus on more self-centred philosophies, how can there be any collective aim other than to collectively aim at not collectively aiming? A strange aim indeed. It is akin to having a car that has a steering wheel for each seat, each connected to its own wheel. This would not be that big of an issue if everyone had the same destination, synchronised their movements and agreed on which route to take to get there. However, if everyone is aiming at different things, has different ideas of how to attain them, and agreed before setting off on their journey that they will aim independently, then this car is going to have all its wheels pointing in different directions. The result will be that no one is going to get to where they want to go, or they are going to end up crashing into a wall. I would argue this same principle applies to families, communities, states, and to nations. If they cannot be united upon fundamental issues, where can they be expected to take themselves except towards disunity and upheaval? The only real question at this point is, when will that disunity occur?

Now I have no knowledge of the future, so any timescales I give would be a complete guess. The consequences of what I have spoken of in this book may come to fruition in my lifetime, it could happen at some point after my

---

46   Pew Research Centre, 'Political Polarization in the American Public, Section 1: Growing Ideological Consistency', *Pew Research Centre*, 12 June 2014,

death, or not at all. Only God knows. The affected societies could, at some point, come to realise the error of their ways. We can take the example of the people of the prophet Yunus (Jonah) who were a people on the brink of destruction, but they were able to change their ways and save themselves from ruin. This may very well occur to modern societies as well, and its consequences could be diverted. The people could begin to aim together at something noble and mend the fractures. However, this change may not occur at all. In which case, only God can really say when such fracturing will eventually take its toll, and how that will unfold.

In Nietzsche's book, *The Gay Science*, in one of the most famous aphorisms he has written titled, "The Madman", he touches on something quite descriptive of this. He describes a man who is known to the townspeople as crazy. He runs into the market square and interrupts the general populous going about their day and minding their own business. He demands to know where God is, and in response they ridicule him. With this, Nietzsche is trying to show how the modern person has lost their faith in God, and see it akin to children's tales, something to laugh at and mock. However, the madman does not take kindly to their mocking him, smashes his lantern on the floor and rebukes them. He makes it very clear that something terrible has occurred and that they do not yet realise the gravity of the situation. At which point he exclaims:

> "'Where is God?' He cried; 'I'll tell you! We have killed him – you and I! We are all his murderers. But how did we do this? How were we able to drink up the sea? Who gave us the sponge to wipe away the entire horizon? What were we doing when we unchained this earth from its sun? Where is it moving to now? Where are we moving to? Away from all suns? Are we not continually falling? And backwards, sidewards, forwards, in all directions? Is there still an up and a down? Aren't we straying as though through an infinite nothing? Isn't empty space breathing at us? Hasn't it got colder? Isn't night and more night coming again and again?"[47]

The killing of God in this paragraph is not meant in a literal sense, but rather it is symbolic of the loss of faith in the Christian world. He talks about the idea of becoming unchained from the sun and drifting out into an infinite void with no sense of direction. Here, the sun is that which everything centres on. So long as we were "chained" to it, we had something we could orbit together that united us, and which gave us direction and light to see.

---

47 Nietzsche F., *The Gay Science*, (Cambridge: Cambridge University Press, 2017) pp. 119-120, [Aphorism #125: The Mad Man].

It was a shared focal reference point. However, after being "unchained", the Christian world had projected us out into an abyss. In a Godless world there is nothing left to keep us centred, give us direction, or light our way.

This being 'thrown out into the darkness' does not necessitate that we float off together either. Each member of the modern society can be left to float in different directions away from each other. It is this that I say is expressive of the modern, secular, and liberal society. An emphasis on freedom and individual unique expression for their own sake, in conjunction with overabundance of choice, information, and the loss of faith in God, is enough to not only unchain us from the sun, but from each other. Therefore, we have the motivating forces in play for the fracturing of society. Everyone is aiming at different ends. What the modern western society considers its highest values necessarily lead to its people drifting apart from one another and becoming alienated. Now, we can no longer even agree on answers to simple question. Who would ever have thought 20 years ago that today we would be watching documentaries of people struggling to explain what a woman is? Who would have guessed that we would repeatedly be handing awards for women over to biological men?

Morality, Meaning & Leaps of Faith

Let us now consider morality and meaning. What role do they play in modern society, which has made a lot of effort to remove God from the social sphere? How does this effect the mental state and the moral thinking of its citizens? Questions on such things as abortion, suicide, sexual identity, race relations, cultural expression, acceptable social behaviours, the role of government or authority, and so on, have a variety of opinions associated with them within the secular western world. If a people cannot be united upon simple things, we cannot expect them to be united on larger and more complex issues, especially without a guiding principle.

If a tradition which binds the people in a society together has been abandoned and replaced with a focus on vague ideas of freedom and personal expression, coupled with such notions as moral relativism or subjectivism, it is no wonder that we see increases in polarisation. If the community at large has valued things which lead that community in countless different directions, can you really expect anything other than increasing political polarisation? If you drill the need to be "unique and individual" into everyone's head enough, it makes sense that many of them would try to go in different directions and to "stand out from the crowd". As time passes and considering the different approaches and outcomes of these ideas to towards growth and development, it appears inevitable that modern secular societies would end up in the current situation. It also seems perfectly reasonable for the average person to look at this quagmire and feel completely overwhelmed and out of their depth. Is it any wonder that such an environment might be the perfect breeding grounds for a societal nihilism? That is, the conditions where the feeling of meaninglessness can become more widespread, causing more confusion and therefore, even more nihilism. A nasty feedback loop indeed.

This now takes us on to a very interesting observation by Nietzsche on the issues with morality following from the "death of God", where the people affected by it have yet to recognise the gravity of the situation:

> "They are rid of the Christian God and now believe all the more firmly that they must cling to Christian morality. [...] In England one must rehabilitate oneself after every little emancipation from theology by showing in a veritably awe-inspiring manner what a moral fanatic one is. That is the penance they pay there.
>
> We others hold otherwise. When one gives up on the Christian faith, one pulls the right to Christian morality from under one's feet. This morality is by no means self-evident: this point has to be exhibited again and again, despite these English flatheads. Christianity is a system, a whole view of things thought out together. By breaking one main concept out of it, the faith in God, one breaks the whole: nothing necessary remains in one's hands. Christianity presupposes that man does not know, cannot know, what is good for him, what evil: he believes in God, who alone knows it. Christianity is a command; its origin is transcendent; it is beyond all criticism, all right to criticism; it has truth if God is the truth – it stands and falls with faith in God.
>
> When the English actually believe that they know "intuitively" what is good and evil, when they therefore suppose that they no longer require Christianity as a guarantee of morality, we merely witness the effects of the dominion of the Christian value-judgement and an expression of the strength and depth of this dominion: such that the origin of English morality has been forgotten, such that the very conditional character of its right to existence is no longer felt. For the English, morality is not yet a problem."[48]

Commitment to higher values are themselves necessarily moral commitments. The commitment is made because a people believe it is *the right thing to do*; a duty because *it is good,* and followed by those in society who are *good*. However, as Nietzsche shows very astutely here, when the morality which has its foundations in the Abrahamic tradition is separated from a belief in God, this also separates it from the necessary moral commitments associated with it. These moral conclusions are by no means "intuitive", but rather they are *inherited*!

The modern secular world has yet to ask why it sees truth as a higher value, or why the society should see itself as having a duty to uphold truth as a necessary value at all. Holding truth in such high regard is a consequence of the Christian roots of the West. But if Christianity has lost its grip on the people and they voluntarily give it up, then the *absolute* commitment

---

48   Nietzsche F., *Twilight of the Idols*, (Oxford: Oxford University Press, 2008), p.45

to truth must be given new justification. The same goes for morality, for reason itself, and to any of the values that society holds. But this raises countless other questions, to which there is an abundance of opinions, and even more information to have to dig through. To who's authority do we abide by? How do we justify and establish this authority that once belonged only to God?

As Nietzsche says, "[d]o we ourselves not have to become gods merely to appear worthy of it?"[49] What do we do when it becomes apparent that such things are absurd to wish for? Furthermore, in a world no longer chained to uniting principles and obsessed with freedom and individualism, to what degree do we apply freedom practically? To what degree do we give up our freedoms for the sake of security and comfort? There is a tension between these two things after all! Freedoms can conflict with one another. My freedom to do something, can take away someone else's freedom from such things. My neighbour's freedom to blast music and party all night with his friends on a weekday takes away my freedom to have a good nights undisturbed sleep.

All of this takes a lot of time, effort, resources, and energy to explore and work out. The average person simply does not have any of this to spare to adequately cover these subjects enough. How can they be expected to make a justified conclusion on these complex matters as a whole? What is left for the busy and ignorant, other than to make huge leaps of faith on the best course of action for us all?

Leaps of faith are absolutely necessary! Be that for the theist or the atheist. Time is constantly steaming ahead and there is nothing we can do to stop it. The necessity to make choices will constantly arise in life, day after day. When this happens, you need to act! Unfortunately, you are not always blessed with time to dwell on it in an armchair and think deeply and philosophically with a team of trained experts. It may be something afforded to the university student in a seminar, but this is not how life plays out for most people.

Take the classical trolley problem thought experiment, which involves deciding whether to pull the lever to prevent the train from killing several people and instead sacrificing only one. Discussions on this one example alone can fill volumes of books which would take more than a lifetime to read, process and contemplate over. However, if this very example were to occur, you would have to decide now! You have no time to think about it endlessly under such circumstances! The train is barrelling down the tracks and if you do not act now, it will be too late. Do you pull the lever

---

49   Nietzsche F., *The Gay Science*, (Cambridge: Cambridge University Press, 2017) pp. 119-120, [Aphorism #125: The Mad Man].

or not? Do you even have time to ask yourself that question? Do you only have the time to act intuitively on an impulse? This is life. Sometimes you may fail to make a choice or refuse to make one, but the outcomes in such circumstances are identical to one of the choices you could have made. Failing to decide actively whether to pull the lever or not has the same outcome as choosing not to pull the lever and letting the five tied to the track perish. Obviously, life is not always as extreme as this thought experiment. However, the underlying theme of having to act now, without having the liberty of much time to contemplate, is a common occurrence in daily life.

This is not to say absolutely everything is a leap of faith, rather it is just to say that leaps of faith occur. Nor is this an attempt to put all knowledge into question. It is simply an attempt to be honest with regards to the limits of the human being. We are not all knowing. We are however, riddled with blind spots and ignorance. Acknowledging this does not necessitate epistemological nihilism[50] as it is itself a knowledge claim. If you admit this, you simultaneously admit you also know something with certainty, and therefore admit knowledge is possible. The point of this is just to acknowledge the necessary starting point for all human beings. It is an attempt to get us to reflect on how our finite nature effects our relationship with the world, with our communities and our place within them. In a faithless society that sees itself as free from God and His commands, that has a focus on vague and poorly defined conceptions of freedom, individualism, materialism, consumerism, and hedonism, there is nothing necessary that binds us together. In the analogy Nietzsche gave, we not only drift away from the sun, but we drift away from almost everything and everyone.

Furthermore, separately from questions of meta-ethics and talks of what "morality" even is, it must first be decided who is put in charge of seeking solutions to these moral problems. However, modern society finds itself in a strange predicament. We have very large populations living in condensed areas. The city of London has nearly 9 million people residing in it.[51] These numbers are so large you cannot even fathom what this would look like as a crowd` stood shoulder to shoulder. To offer some perspective, Wembley Stadium, the largest stadium in London, can hold 90,000 people. You would need 100 of these stadiums to hold the population of the entire city! This is huge! How does this group of people decide who should run the city in

---

50   Epistemology is the study of knowledge, and "epistemological nihilism" is specifically a position that negates the possibility of achieving any true knowledge. It is a pessimistic relationship towards our ability to attain truths about ourselves and the world.
51   Data Commons Team, 'Data Commons Timeline: London Population', *Data commons,*

a way that doesn't require leaps of faith, or trust in large groups of strangers? It's impossible. Faith and trust in strangers who have faith and trust in strangers is an inevitable part of the process. A city of 9 million people cannot know each other intimately enough to say they know the people who run their city "well enough" so that it doesn't constitute faith. Especially if many of them don't even know their own next-door neighbours!

The reality is that our condition is such that we have no choice but to initiate systems of faith that we believe best mediate these epistemological issues. This is not to say we should just throw them all out of the window and cease to use them because we found that "dirty word". Faith is an inescapable part of life; I accept and understand that and so should you. However, I see it is a growing issue that many fail to see the necessity of faith in everyday life on many occasions and naively reject this fact. Ironically, some people have faith in the idea that they don't have faith; or that faith is somehow synonymous with being "backwards" and lacking critical thinking skills. This is far from the truth.

I will now begin to develop our understanding towards a cure for this sickness. I will explore the cyclical condition. Despite those effected by nihilism rejecting religion and traditional values, they still end up looking to them for ideas and practices to make up for the void they have been left with because of that rejection. I call this the Nihilist yearning. I certainly hope that a deeper exploration of this subject area will help us to understand how nihilism has managed to take as much of a hold on society as it has done, and God willing, help us to understand how to overcome it.

The Nihilist Yearning

In an article written by Alain de Botton about why he believes that Science could "at last, properly replace Religion", he writes how "we are – in a glorious and redemptive way – what we always feared: nothing."[52] Despite this being a clear oxymoron, individuals like this perpetuate the significance of the insignificance of the human being, and so perpetuate nihilism even further. The author runs a popular YouTube channel called "The School of Life", which has nearly 6 *million* subscribers! He is also the author of a book called "Religion for Atheists: A non-believer's guide to the uses of religion", which admittedly takes a positive look at religion, but is still underpinned by atheism and the nihilistic tendency of reducing the human being to nothing, and then tries to lead the reader to a sense of self-determined purpose and significance. Which is effectively telling someone there is no water, and then leading them to a water hole with no water in it to "quench their thirst".

Despite this commitment to nihilism and inclination to atheism, people are still seeing the benefits of religion. They pick and choose what suits them from it to make up for what they have come to lack in their rejection of it; a type of "pick & mix" religion. We see similar trends in the New Atheism movement, with characters like Sam Harris increasingly making attempts to take what he sees as beneficial from religion. This can be found throughout his book entitled "Waking Up: A Guide to Spirituality Without Religion", going as far as incorporating religious practices with a new atheist twist. Interestingly, in an article written by the guardian, Harris is quoted saying: "We need to live our lives with more than just understanding facts. Not being wrong is not the ultimate state of being for people in this life."[53] Related to this same idea, in an interview with the online publication New

---

52   de Botton A., "How Science Could – at Last – Properly Replace Religion", *The School of Life*,
53   Anthony A., 'Sam Harris, the new atheist with a spiritual side', *The Guardian*, 16 February 2019,

Scientist, Alain de Botton was asked the following:

> "Your opening gambit in your new book, *Religion for Atheists*, is to say, of course religions are not true, and you leave it at that. Does the question not interest you?"

To which de Botton answered:

> "No, because I think most of us don't make up our minds in a rational way. You don't say "I'm an atheist because I've looked at all the evidence and this is what I think." Similarly, you don't say "I'm religious because I've surveyed all the evidence.""[54]

How interesting. We have here what can only be described as a leap of faith. That is, to commit to something without necessarily having all the available evidence, and not even being bothered enough to explore it. It seems to be conceded here that it's a necessary move for those who choose to incline to the ideas stated in his work. Especially when they have goals that undermine themselves and no definite thing to aim at. The only other options are heedless hedonism to avoid confrontation with these issues, or suicide, which as we see from the statistics shared earlier, is becoming increasingly more troubling.

As Nietzsche encapsulates perfectly in his aphorism of the madman, where he boldly claims that we are the murderers responsible for the "death of God", this has resulted in our becoming a rootless people. He describes this act as analogous to, and I paraphrase, 'drinking up the sea' or 'wiping away the horizon with a sponge'. That is, he is trying to get across the point that we have somehow achieved the impossible. He further expands on this point by saying that we have 'unchained the earth from its sun', and now must deal with floating through an abyss without any sense of direction or perspective; with no points by which to orient ourselves.[55]

I find this to be a very poetic way of describing the loss of a people's foundation when they have disconnected themselves to the very thing that grounded them. Like a tree that destroys its own roots with the hope of becoming a greater tree, only to collapse under its own weight and rot. Prior to "the death of God", what offered the people meaning and direction was their tradition; their belief in a higher purpose and power. But upon losing that, what was left to keep them upright and firm? The answer: nothing.

---

54 Lawton G., "The God issue: Alain de Botton's religion for atheists", *NewScientist*, 14 March 2012,

55 Nietzsche F., *The Gay Science*, (Cambridge: Cambridge University Press, 2017) pp. 119-120, [Aphorism #125: The Mad Man].

As was clearly asked in the 'madman' quote, is there still an up or a down? How do you determine values anymore? With the loss of any religion or tradition, you necessarily lose the values which were underpinned by it. Some bury their heads in the sand and try to ground it in other things without consensus, desperately attempting to keep a hold of the values they inherited. But up to now all we seem to have been able to do is create an increasingly polarised society. This polarisation appears to be fuelled by an emphasis on individuality and freedom of personal expression over and above that of communal values. Although, paradoxically, this emphasis has itself become a communal value, and has thus become another higher value that undermines itself.

Furthermore, Nietzsche alludes to something else incredibly interesting. In analysing the seriousness of the situation with regards to the loss of faith in God, he says: "Do we not ourselves have to become gods to appear worthy of it?" This doesn't need to be taken in the literal sense, in that we need to become like the mythological characters found in the Greek or Roman pantheons for example, but it can be again looked at in terms of higher values. Where God was once that which occupied the highest place in our hierarchy of values, after losing faith, the people replace Him with themselves. Either the community is made the highest value as you see expressed in extreme forms of nationalism or communism, or the individual makes themselves a god insofar as they see themselves as their own highest value. In making themselves the highest value, so are the related values that stem from this, such as their desires, their wants, and their needs.

Echoing once again the words I previously quoted from the YouTube channel Kurzgesagt, "If our life is all we get to experience, then it's the only thing that matters. If the universe has no principles, the only principles relevant are the ones *we* decide on." Instead of the laws being dictated upon us by a higher and wiser being, namely God, we have been left with nothing but ourselves. As de Botton has already alluded to, this is to be left with nothing at all.

If religion, defined vaguely, is the accepted rulings given by an ultimate authority, and in a nihilistic framework there is no ultimate authority above your own,[56] then the nihilist hasn't escaped religion. Instead, they become the authors of their own religion. They are left to decide for themselves whether they wish to obey the authority of others or not, whether they are willing to experience the difficulties that follow the rejection of the authority of others, and what rituals they wish to perform. You need to look no further than the popular atheists to see the attempts to build replacement communities that can compete with openly religious ones.

---

56   Unless suppressed by some form of power imbalance by others.

They have their replacements for the high priests, who have adoring fans and are looked up to as ambiguous guides. Richard Dawkins is one such figure. His bestselling book *The God Delusion* has sold millions of copies and receives countless praises by his fans. They seem to be completely unaware of the devastating critiques of his work by philosophers of science like Michael Ruse, who said:

> "Unlike the new atheists, I take scholarship seriously. I have written that *The God Delusion* made me ashamed to be an atheist and I meanit."[57]

Why, despite critiques like this and other critiques, do people still take his half-baked ideas seriously, is beyond me. The only explanation I can give is that they are enamoured by his rhetoric.

As I stated earlier, the human being, by its very nature, is a purpose driven being. The psychologist and philosopher Viktor Frankl says that "[m]an's search for meaning is the primary motivation in his life and not a "secondary rationalisation" of instinctual drives."[58] The nihilism I have been focusing on throughout this book is not only the reasoned philosophical notion of nihilism, but also the psychological condition, the pathological state, and the mental exhaustion that express themselves as feelings of meaninglessness. If Frankl is correct in his evaluation of mankind it follows that just as the sick person seeks a cure for their disease and yearns for it with all their being, then so too does the one stricken by nihilism. With the decline of religious belief around the world and with an increase in atheism/agnosticism,[59] it makes sense that you would see a type of religious behaviour manifest in their attempts to flee nihilism and fill the voids that have been left in their rejection of their previous traditions.

---

[57] Ruse M., 'Dawkins et al bring us into disrepute', *The Guardian*, 2 November 2009,

[58] Frankl V. E., *Man's Search for Meaning*, (London: Rider, 2004), p.105.

[59] Pew Research Centre, 'The Changing Global Religious Landscape', *Pew Research Centre*, 5 April 2017, p.17.

PART 3

Overcoming Obstacles

What Obstacles?

The task of what follows now is to put Islam forward as an antidote to the nihilistic issues faced by modern society. I do intend to do this with respect to both the causes and effects of nihilism, however, before I can do this effectively, I will need to offer responses to some common objections that act as a barrier to people taking Islam as a serious option. This is often because of misconceptions picked up by popular atheist apologetics. Just as someone who is against vaccines may prevent themselves from obtaining a legitimate cure to their ailments, I will attempt to show how these common objections act in a very similar manner. The arguments I discuss herein are often put forward by detractors of Islam (and other religions), yet they fail to offer any valid reasons to avoid studying and to continue dismissing it. God willing, I hope that in tackling these issues first, I may be able to carve a clear path through the confusing overgrowth that exists in today's anti-religious polemics. So, without further ado, let us jump straight into it.

Why Believe in the Divine?

Why should we believe in the divine? Is it not more natural to take an atheistic position? The short answer is no, not at all. Belief in the supernatural comes very naturally to the human being. An article written by Paul Bloom (a "self-declared atheist"[60]) titled *Religion is Natural*, makes the case that "recent findings suggest that two foundational aspects of religious belief —belief in mind-body dualism [the existence of a soul], and belief in divine agents— come naturally to young children",[61] and this is the case even if the parents that raise them do not share this belief.[62] God says in the Qur'an:

> And [remember] when your Lord brought forth from the loins of the children of Adam their descendants and had them testify regarding themselves. [Allah asked,] "Am I not your Lord?" They replied, "Yes, You are! We testify." [He cautioned,] "Now you have no right to say on the Day of Judgment, 'We were not aware of this.'"[63]

All of this adds credence to the Islamic idea of the fitrah, which is the notion that belief in God and the supernatural is innately ingrained into our very being.[64] Richard Dawkins even concedes that historically there has never been an atheist civilisation. When asked on Joe Rogan's podcast, "has there ever been a civilisation that existed without a belief in a higher power?", his response was "I don't think there has, no."[65] The divine has

---

60   Rothenberg Gritz J., 'Wired for Creationism', *The Atlantic*, December 2005,
61   Bloom P., 'Religion is natural', Developmental *Science*, 10/1, (2007), 147-151 (p.147).
62   ibid, p.150.
63   The Clear Qur'an, Trans by Dr M. Khattab, 7:172
64   Hamza Tzortzis also dedicated chapter 4 of his book, *The Divine Reality*, to bolster this point: Tzortzis H. A., *The Divine Reality: God, Islam & The Mirage of Atheism*, (Lion Rock Publishing, 2019) pp. 67-79.
65   Rogan J. & Dawkins R., '#1366 - Richard Dawkins', *The Joe Rogan Experience*,

always been a constant feature throughout human history and continues to be so today. Furthermore, Jamie Turner has put forward a convincing case defending the proposition that "theistic belief can be properly basic". That is to say that belief in God can be rational without argumentation. In fact, he has also argued that this can be specifically applied to full-fledged Islamic belief as well.[66]

As Allah says in the Qur'an:

> "So be steadfast in faith in all uprightness [O Prophet]—the natural Way of Allah which He has instilled in [all] people. Let there be no change in this creation of Allah. That is the Straight Way, but most people do not know."[67]

God has placed in each human being the ability to recognise His existence. God is not an elitist and has not made it necessary for every human being to have to jump through endless complex philosophical hoops to come to the realisation of His existence. Recognition of this fact should be just as accessible to the farmer as it is to the academic. Allah says, "We have sent you (O Prophet) only as a mercy for the whole world",[68] not just a few clever people with the time and ability to tackle countless abstract ideas and arguments. To suggest otherwise is unreasonable.

---

21 October 2019, timestamp: 38 mins.

66   In short, this idea is grounded on the notion that we have, what has been coined, "basic beliefs", i.e., beliefs that we don't hold based on any other beliefs. Given the fulfilment of certain epistemic conditions, these basic beliefs can be "properly basic." That is, basic and rational. Turner has argued extensively for an application of these epistemic principles to theistic and Islamic belief in the following essay published by the Sapience Institute: Turner J., 'Who Shoulders the Burden of Proof? Reformed Epistemology & Properly Basic Islamic Belief', *Sapience Institute*, 9 December 2020,

67   The Clear Quran, 30:30

68   Ibid., 21:107

No Empirical Evidence?

Another common tactic is the demand for direct empirical evidence of God's existence. I would like to give you a very simple example which should be sufficient to show the absurdity of such a request. Consider this: one day I make a computer game with self-aware artificial intelligence contained within it. They have an ingrained belief programmed into them which makes belief in a higher power completely natural. However, one day, one of them begins to doubt and demands evidence for the creator. He insists that he limits what will be accepted as evidence to material things contained within the computer game. Can you see why this might be absurd? He is essentially demanding you show him the game developer inside of the game. This is like demanding to see evidence of the painter but limiting the evidence to the painting itself. Such unreasonable demands can never be fulfilled, and the inability to meet this demand is not sufficient for them to claim justification in their denial of that which comes innately to all societies, nor of that which is inferred by the existence of all things.

It is important to establish what should be considered evidence. Sometimes when in dialogue (with atheists/agnostics) in particular, you may come across someone who demands direct empirical evidence exclusively and completely neglect all the other types of evidence available that could be completely relevant to many different contexts. Here are a few examples:

1. **Rational evidence**: This refers to arguments and logical reasoning which can be used to support claims where empirical evidence is difficult or impossible to obtain. This could involve using deductive reasoning to try and make inferences to conclusions from a string of true premises, inductive reasoning to try and make generalisations from sets of data, or abductive reasoning which involves coming up with hypotheses or explanations which are based on incomplete/uncertain information, and you try to fill in the gaps. Other than this you have analogical reasoning, causal reasoning, and counterfactual reasoning, just to name a few.

2. **Testimonial evidence:** This can include things like the statements of reliable and trustworthy witnesses, and expert testimony from those trained in or familiar with certain fields. All of these can and do offer great insight in many circumstances and is even heavily used within the scientific community. Every scientist does not take it upon themselves to replicate every single scientific experiment to consider themselves capable of referencing it or utilising it in their own work or thinking. When reading a scientific paper, you are taking the testimony of those who have claimed to do the experimentation so that you don't have to. All of this can give you great insight and perspective that you may not have achieved from direct empirical evidence, especially considering you may not actually have the expertise to be able to understand or interpret that evidence even if it was presented to you.

3. **Circumstantial evidence**: This can be a kind of evidence that may not necessarily be a direct and indisputable proof of a particular claim, but it can be something which can be brought forward as supporting the increased likelihood of one claim over other competing claims. Let me give you an example. If you find someone's DNA at a crime scene, you can use this circumstantial evidence to build a case against them as a potential suspect. It would certainly give you good reason to suspect them over others whose DNA was not present and can be used as evidence despite not being bulletproof. As yes, it may increase the weight of one claim over another, but it doesn't guarantee that claims truth. Nonetheless, the fact that it is not an absolute proof is not enough to dismiss its utility.

4. **Anecdotal evidence**: This has a bit of overlap with testimonial evidence, and includes stories and experiences given by individuals which has the potential to offer valuable insight into certain issues or phenomenon. This one is one that can be criticised for being unreliable, but nonetheless it can be useful when it comes to trying to understand subjective experiences of people and the ways that they can be impacted by these events.

5. **Statistical evidence**: This is the analysis of data and information to find insight into trends, patterns or relationships between things that could potentially be missed, or not be completely obvious from the start when relying on things like direct observations alone.

Understanding that there are many different types of evidence, and that most of these can and are used in a variety of different contexts is incredibly important. They are crucial not just when we are talking specifically about things like religion, but also when it comes to many other fields outside of this too. For example, the scientific community can and does understand the limits and sometimes the strengths offered by varying types of evidence. It is important when it comes to constructing or designing the way experiments may be conducted, or when analysing the data or drawing conclusions from the information that has been gathered. Outside of science, such evidence is used in politics or in courts of law. It is very important that we recognise and make the effort to utilise the different types of evidence which are available when it is suitable to do so according to the context. Let us not be those who completely neglect to consider the nuances of this subject matter and stop asking for evidence of the baker inside of the bread.

Too Many Gods & Religions!

A common objection to the theistic position is merely to point to the sheer number of gods and religions in existence around the world today and throughout history. This is important as it is connected to one of the major contributing factors that give rise to the experience of nihilism (as I outlined earlier). That is, nihilism being brought on as the result of being overwhelmed by large amounts of information. In short, I explained how this generates hopelessness, which in turn leads to a belief that the task at hand is one which is impossible to conquer. Life is short, and the mountain of information you must consume is too large. What follows from this is the loss of any motivation to tackle the issues at hand. It is to fall into *apathetic agnosticism* and ceasing to care about what the answers to many of the big questions are. But this path to the rejection of religion wholesale is not justifiable. It fails to ask if there are any methods which we can use to help us sort through large amounts of information in an effective way. For example, let us say that someone has been murdered, and Sherlock Holmes deduces the possibility of it being 1 of 3 suspects based on the available evidence. Would I be justified in barging into the investigation and exclaiming:

> "Oh my! How are we ever going to find the murderer!? Never mind these 3 people or whether there is good reason to take them as potential suspects! There are 8 billion people on the planet, and it could have been any one of them! We cannot make a conclusion until we have assessed every single person individually! But as this is an impossible task, we should not bother to investigate at all!"

Would anyone really be justified in using this to stop the investigation? Of course not! Furthermore, it would be even more absurd to go a step further and deny the existence of a murderer altogether, simply because the quantity of potential candidates and information is so large. It should not be (falsely) assumed that we would have to explore every conceivable possibility to come to a justified conclusion. That is, convict someone of a crime.

When I began my journey into religious discourse, I found myself often overwhelmed by the sheer number of different religions and all the different approaches to religious discourse. I used the fact that I was overwhelmed by the number of possibilities as a quasi-refutation to all religions. I would echo the words of the likes of Richard Dawkins and his ilk, who perpetrate such thinking. They do this every time they point to the large numbers of religions as one of many reasons that lead to the rejection of religion altogether. Just as in the absurd example of someone who might reject the existence of a murderer despite the clear signs available to the contrary, I truly believe people reject the Creator along the same lines. Dawkins repeats this cliche often enough that he seems to believe that the argument has some merit. Enough so for it to be his opening statement on his feature of his *Big Think* discussion on "Faith".[69] But is it really a good objection?

We must first ask ourselves, are there any good methods available to help us sift through this very large pile of information? And if there was, would this make this very objection a moot point? Do we really need to research every religion, *in full,* to justifiably be able to pick one of them?

Let us return for a moment, to the example of the murderer. One way we can overcome this trivial issue is to ask certain questions which will reduce the number of suspects by placing them into categories that can then be written off and anything that falls into that category can be disregarded. For example, if the murder took place in Scotland, from this one piece of information alone we do not even need to consider anyone who has never been to Scotland. You can further reduce the number of suspects by asking more questions and through a process of elimination be left with a much more manageable figure that is not nearly as daunting as the first. Furthermore, if you have evidence or reasons that give you good justification for taking something seriously, then you might not even need to go through the process of elimination. For example, if you had a confession from someone who had the murder weapon, had motive, had the ability, and fits

---

69   In response to the question "When did you first realize you were an atheist?", Richard Dawkins responds by saying: "I think first the realisation that there are lots of different religions and they can't all be right and the Christian one in which I was brought up was clearly only one of many. But that didn't finally make me into an atheist. What finally made me into an atheist was the realisation that there was no scientific reason to believe in any sort of supernatural creator, and that came with the understanding of Darwinian evolution." - Dawkins R., "Richard Dawkins: Faith | Big Think", *Big Think*, 2 Jun 2011, YouTube,

the crime perfectly, then you can close the case and cease investigations.

The same can be done with religion. We can place them into categories and ask questions about the fundamentals of these categories. We can deliberate between them about which is more likely to be true and which is the most rationally coherent option.

Apostates from many religions often complain about being told you need to have something equivalent to a PhD in a religion to leave it but need no good reason at all to join the fold. However, I would argue that just as you do not necessarily need a PhD to leave a religion, neither do you need one to join; and by greater reason, you certainly do not need one in every religion out there to decide. This is not to say that you do not need valid reasons to join a religion. I stand firmly in the belief that if you affirm something for the wrong reasons, even if it happens to be true, that it can potentially be detrimental to that person when it comes to maintaining that belief. Later down the line they may discover issues with the reasons that motivated accepting a proposition, and this could stimulate abandoning the belief altogether. I have witnessed this many times and had to speak to people who have made this mistake.[70] This would clearly be a tremendous loss if the abandoned belief was true. So, for this reason, I advise everyone to think carefully and sincerely about these things.

What questions could be asked then? You could begin with the most fundamental question: Is there a God? If, in your exploration of the subject you conclude that the answer to this question is yes or no, then you can disregard everything that falls under the incorrect answer. This is exactly what atheists do when they disregard all religions (as they conclude the answer to the question is no). But let us for a moment assume that the arguments atheists have against the notion of a God ultimately fail upon further analysis, does that mean that you cannot continue to use this method? Of course not. It simply means the process of questioning continues. If throughout this exploration we become convinced of a creative agent, we can continue to ask about its nature. Is it more likely to have a will, or be equivalent to a mindless machine churning out multiple universe? Is it better to refer to this creative force as a singular being or as a multiplicity? Upon going down this line of questioning, you can effectively write off large numbers of religions. If it can be shown through this exploration, for example, that pure monotheism is the most coherent option, then what need is there to continue looking into the countless polytheistic pantheons that do and have existed historically? If it can also be shown that these

---

70   This has been via the Lighthouse Mentoring project offered by Sapience Institute where I have spoken to hundreds of people concerning their doubts about Islam. (www.sapienceinstitute.org/lighthouse)

polytheistic positions presuppose a unique, singular creative force that then gives rise to any multiplicity, then we can just focus specifically on monotheistic religions. Asking these very fundamental questions is an incredibly effective method of sorting through the available information, and simply pointing out the sheer number of religions is not a valid rebuttal, as it can easily be overcome.

Let us now posit a sceptic that is not completely satisfied but they are willing to concede (for the sake of argument) to the monotheistic position being more rational than a polytheistic one. However, they still insist on asking: "which One God is the right one? Is it the God of the Jews? The God of the Christians? The God of the Muslims?" The assumption here is that because each monotheistic party describe their God in different ways, that this necessarily means that each claim must refer to some unique entity rather than simply being a mixture of true and false descriptions of the same one God.

I will give the example of a man, let us call him Dave. He has connections with three different people. Each connection was established at a different time, and these three acquaintances meet up and describe Dave differently. The first says that Dave is X and the second says that Dave is not X. The third says Dave is Y and the first denies it and says Dave is not Y. However, despite all their disagreements, there is a lot of overlap on things they do agree on. For example, each of the three people understand Dave to be a builder and to have been responsible for building a particular house. They all consider him to be a good and competent builder responsible for its creation and admit that this house belongs to him.

A fourth person then joins the conversation. He listens to them talk and notices that each of them has a different way of referring to the mutual friend; one calls him Dave, another David, and the last Davey. He then notices the disagreement about the description of certain attributes held by the mutual friend. He hears someone say that Dave loves everyone he ever meets, regardless of what kind of person they are. He hears the next disagree and say that is not true, he knows Dave does not love evil people, but despite this, he is the most loving person he has ever come across and is always open to forgiving those who seek forgiveness. He then hears another debate about whether Dave is capable of being a married bachelor or not. The debates continue and as a result the fourth member claims they must all be talking about a different person. He asks: "Which Dave is the right Dave?" And due to the existence of these differences, insists he lacks belief in all three Dave's because of the incorrect inference that each description is of a different person. As Allah says in the Qur'an:

«We believe in what has been revealed to us and what was revealed to you. Our God and your God is (only) One. And to Him we (fully) submit.»[71]

The fact that others describe Him incorrectly, or associate things with him incorrectly, does not make their God a different God, in the same way as the example above shows that people making false descriptions about someone is not enough to say they are talking about different people. It can simply mean that one or more of the people that are describing said person have made a mistake in their evaluation.

To conclude this section, it is not enough to point to the large number of religions, or gods, or even to the differing descriptions of what is referred to as "The One God", to refute the idea of religion or of God. It is characteristic of impatience and laziness more than it is intellectual rigour. There are valid methods that can and should be utilised to overcome the objections given. These methods are used by many people to deduce which religion is the right religion, and what understanding of God is best.

---

[71] Qur'an, 29:46.

On the Wisdom of Old

It is not unreasonable to suggest that tradition can sometimes be a bad thing. Allah makes this clear in the Qur'an when He chastises people for holding on to something simply because they found their fathers following it.[72] Abraham is shown to be someone who breaks away from the way of his people and suffers the consequences of that decision. They are so displeased with his unwillingness to follow what his forefathers were upon that they attempt to burn him in a fire. Islam opens itself up to the necessity of critiquing certain traditions because of their content and rejects them on this basis. However, this is not a rejection of tradition wholesale. Tradition in this framework is not seen as bad by virtue of the fact that it is a tradition, but rather because of that which it wishes to instil in its people; the worship of anything other than the one true God.

Now beyond the notion of associating partners with Allah and committing what is referred to as "shirk" in the Islamic paradigm, tradition can be seen as something that is possibly useful for a people and not something to be taken away if it cannot be replaced with something better. In Islamic lands there were a class of people known as *dhimmīs*, or "protected people".[73] These people, as the name suggests, were given protection under Islamic rule. They were allowed to practise their traditions and to live within their communities unharmed. The value of having a tradition rather than nothing at all and an understanding of the importance of this to a people is inferred within the rulings of Islamic law. There can be genuinely productive practices separated from the acts of worship to other than God, that can develop and become imbedded as part of a culture. These practices can be derived through a process of trial and error, and you may see the benefits of them either immediately, or in the long run. Some of the benefits of such practices could be so subtle that many may not be able to see them at all.

---

72   Qur'an, 21:53, 26:74, 43:22.
73   Alkiek T., "Religious Minorities Under Muslim Rule", *Yaqeen Institute for Islamic Research*, 8 Feb 2017,

Take preventative measures as an example. If there is a particular kind of behaviour that gives rise to problematic consequences on a societal level, if not kept in check, and these problems only slowly manifested after several generations, then it is conceivable that preventative measures that are put in place could stop the possibility of these problems from manifesting. However, it would also prevent the populous from seeing or experiencing the consequences of removing such restrictions and therefore they would not see or experience the benefits of it either. In this way they become blind to its benefits because its presence is something they were born into and raised within.

I have a great example of this with the blessings we have bestowed upon us today, and I will use this to draw an analogy with the restrictive nature of tradition. There was a time when our ancestors did not have access to washing machines. There are still people in certain parts of the world that do not have such luxuries today. Instead, they must clean their clothes by hand, sometimes having to travel down to the local river to do so. The methods they apply in the absence of these luxuries require a lot of effort and energy. This is effort and energy we no longer need to worry about because technological advancements have removed these problems from our lives. However, it is seldom you hear about someone who gazes upon their washing machine with awe, or any common household device for that matter. These things have become peripheral. Like the air that we breath, we barely take notice of it until its existence (or lack thereof) becomes a problem. For example, when it malfunctions and ceases to do what it is supposed to do. At this point, it can become a burden and a source of stress. Once it is fixed, very quickly falls back into the peripheral of our daily experiences. It is a tool. We throw our washing in, we hit some buttons, and we go about our daily lives. The same could be said about many things we have in our households: refrigerators, flushing toilets, running clean water, central heating, the internet etc. All these things are luxuries, especially when you take a perspective which includes the standards of living throughout all of history. We have plenty of reasons to be infinitely grateful for our current situations; we live even better than kings did, just a century ago.

If you take someone who has lived without knowledge of the existence of such luxuries and give it to them, it is likely that the awe and appreciation that they experience would arrive almost immediately. However, contrast that with the likes of the modern individual, born and raised with such things around them for generations. It can hardly be said to register as an experience, or as something significant at all. Its very existence and the fact that it is functioning well are things which are expected. Unless it becomes a problem, at which point such blessings become annoying, and fixing it only gives us relief.

Now to draw this back to the idea of the restrictive nature of tradition.[74] The negative effects that certain restrictions keep at bay will not be noticed by virtue of the fact that they are kept at bay. If you do not experience a problem, you have no necessary trigger to make you aware of its existence. In the same way that I said the existence of the washing machine becomes peripheral and that the problems in life that are caused by the removal of the tool are hidden due to it working as it should, this can also occur to the tradition. The benefits of the restriction can become peripheral and cease to be noticed by those who benefit from them. They become nothing more than the whirring of a washing machine in the background of a noisy home.

For example, let us say there is a hypothetical society that does not allow the wide-spread drinking of alcohol, and the people that make up this society are not aware of the long-term negative effects that take hold of the society, who allow such things to occur. To transition from treating such things as taboo to then allowing them to occur out of ignorance of its consequences, is going to expose this society to a lot of problems that they could have otherwise avoided. In the UK for example:

> "Alcohol is implicated in an enormous amount of crime and disorder, and the effects on victims can be devastating. It is a factor of around 39% of all violent crimes in England and 49% in Wales, as well as contributing to public disorder and anti-social behaviour in communities across the country."[75]

Keeping alcohol out of a society is one way of preventing the consequences caused by it, which include the unnecessary strain mentioned above, but also much more. It is said that the direct costs of alcohol use to the government amount to around £3.9 billion per annum, which is spent on the NHS, police, criminal justice system, and welfare system.[76][77]

---

74 By restrictions, I refer to the laws, or code of conduct, which makes a command of those under its influence. In Islam for example, sexual relations outside of a recognised and legal marriage are considered impermissible. Anything beyond this is *restricted*.

75 Alcohol Change UK, 'Alcohol Statistics', *Alcohol Change UK*,

76 One of the main reasons this is allowed to continue is because money made from alcohol taxation amounts to over £10 billion, and it is seen as economically profitable. But to look at this only in terms of its monetary pros and cons completely neglects the individuals, families and communities that have had their lives destroyed by addiction, crime, neglect and more.

77 Snowden C., "Alcohol and the Public Purse: Do drinkers pay their way?",

This is where the importance of taking tradition seriously must be stressed. We should not be rejecting tradition because it is considered restrictive, without asking questions about what harm those restrictions are preventing. Additionally, we certainly should not be rejecting it simply by virtue of it being a tradition. The fact that something is old is not enough to deduce that it is foolish, and the fact that something is meant to restrict you from a particular kind of behaviour is not enough to call it "oppressive". When I tell my daughter not to put forks in the plug socket, I am not acting like an unruly dictator making arbitrary decisions absent of any wisdom. On the contrary, I care for her wellbeing and wish to facilitate an environment that is conducive to her flourishing, regardless of whether she can understand my reasoning or not.

Another common objection against tradition is the notion that "we should be allowed to learn from our own mistakes." However, this should not be put forward without regard for when such a notion might be suitable, and when not. It might very well be fair enough to say this when your child is going through a process of trial and error while learning how to play chess, or building a small robot, but it certainly would not be a praiseworthy approach if they are thinking of trying heroin or drinking bleach. I think many would agree that in such circumstances, it is perfectly reasonable for the older and wiser to step in and prevent them from making a mistake. Especially when the "lessons" may cause lasting harm or even death. It is better to demand that the individual in question looks at the experiences of others, and learns from their mistakes; rather than having to make their own, or simply to trust those who have more life experience and who care for them. Yes, it is true that going through the process of making that mistake might give you a deeper insight into the wisdom behind the need for a restriction, but it certainly is not necessary. Also, there is not much insight to be had if something kills you or harms you in a significant way. The wise can learn from the mistakes of others, and do not need to make the mistakes themselves. Learning from others also saves time and allows it to be spent on more productive endeavours. This is what is expressed when we say that we are "standing on the shoulders of giants". We do not need to go through the difficulties our predecessors did. Magnus Carlsen, a Norwegian Chess world champion, was able to surpass many of his competitors from a very early age because he had the ability to get a head start on consuming the techniques of the other grand-masters and not have to make the same mistakes they did to get to their level. He could just review their greatest games, take what was good and leave what wasn't.

IEA Discussion Paper No.63, Institute of Economic Affairs,

Tradition can conceivably be the wisdom of the old, and a call from the people of ages gone by, advising us to avoid certain types of behaviour in the same way that I may command my daughter not to put a fork in the plug socket. Tradition can be the process of learning from the mistakes of others who have more wisdom, gained by a collection of experiences. Tradition could also conceivably be handed down from a higher power with the wisdom, knowledge, and ability to give us guidance so that we do not have to make the mistakes others have made or will make. This could be to protect us from harm, or to simply give us a competitive edge against other people or systems of thought. We must stand in the possibility that there may very well be something to learn from the stories we are given, but this involves a mindful exploration, not a mindless rejection. I want you, the reader, to begin an exploration into Islam. Be open to the possibility of the wisdom available within its teachings.

More on Leaps of Faith

Earlier in the book, we discussed how life is short and time passes quickly. Unfortunately, we do not have the ability to stop time from barrelling forward and to ponder on the problems of life until we feel we have pondered on them enough. Unlike the typical thought experiments given in philosophy seminars, where we are given a particular example of a problem and have hours to discuss this with classmates, lecturers and friends, this luxury is not always provided in the real world. Sometimes a dilemma arises, and it demands a response from you *now*. A child may be drowning, but you do not have the time to consider whether the child may grow to be the next Adolf Hitler. Nor do you have the time to consider whether your action is good because of its consequences or because of the intention, or whether something is good by its nature or because it was commanded etc. Sometimes you just have to act! Time keeps moving forward, and for the theist and the atheist it demands the occasional leap of faith. We are ignorant beings who lack a complete picture. We do not ever have all the information at hand in any given moment. Despite this however, we must still make choices; we must still act. Even refusing to act in a positive sense (that is, to *do something*) is to act in a negative sense (to *do nothing*).

One of the definitions of faith is to have "great trust or confidence in something or someone".[78] It can also mean to have "belief that is not based on proof",[79] or held without question. Many of the actions we take daily are based on leaps of faith. We often have trust or confidence in both the things we do, and the people we depend on throughout society; whether proof is available or not. Seldom do we question it. We do not have food testers making sure our food is not poisoned; we do not check every bank note and coin we are given to make sure they are legitimate; we believe that the sun will rise tomorrow; we continue to make plans as though we will continue to exist; we pick jobs and career paths that we do not yet

---

78 "Faith", Cambridge Dictionary, Cambridge University Press,
79 "Faith", Dictionary.com, 2023,

have any experience in; we trust the drivers on the road will not swerve and crash into us while we walk along the pavement; we commit to long term relationships and start families despite having no vision of how the future will turn out. The list goes on.

More importantly however (and we mentioned this briefly in the section above on empirical evidence) is the confidence, trust and faith people have in the scientific community, as well as the relationship the scientific community has with the public and among themselves. Every individual must specialise in something, and the consequence of this specialisation is to have hyper focus in a single slice of one or maybe several fields out of many. Take the physicist for example, he must first pick a subject to focus on. In this case that would be physics. Once he has picked his subject, he will then further specialise as his studies in this field progress. He must focus on something specific, like Quantum mechanics or Astrophysics, which he will then further specialise in again. Each branch of science leads to more branches, like a tree. Each branch has an abundance of information that anyone who specialises in it needs to absorb to grasp the field and become competent in it. As an individual, you must focus on what is at hand, and maybe read summaries, or brief explanations of connecting or parallel fields. Everyone will have a greater grasp of their own chosen fields and must have trust and confidence in the community they are embedded within at large. That is, they do not have the time or the ability to check that everyone is doing as they should be, and not making mistakes or being negligent. Nor do they have time to check for corruption and wrongdoing. This is the case for every individual in the larger community. If you were to draw this out in a diagram, and from every individual you draw a line in blue to show what they have knowledge in and what evidence they have observed, and a red line for everything they have trust or confidence in without being shown the evidence, then you would see that the diagram would have a lot more red-lines in it than blue as a consequence of this specialisation. Now if you then continue to overlay the maps of all people involved in this complex and intricate network of learning and knowledge, you will come to see that the red lines (indicating faith) would come to dominate the diagram to the point where very little blue would be seen at all, if any. This isn't to say the things they have faith in have no validity or basis for them, it is simply to point out that faith exists in the communities, despite what the nay-sayers may insist.

The major issue here is that no one can oversee this entire operation as it is too large and complex. No one has the entire thing grasped. We believe in it pragmatically because what we are doing seems to produce results.[80]

---

80   By "results" we mean progress in technological output and the advancements

Faith is an intricate part of society. The modern machine has become so complex, and so intricate, that it seems to be completely inevitable and necessary.

My aim with this section is to put forward the proposition that it makes no sense to ridicule faith. This is especially so considering that it is an integral part of human life and a necessary consequence of our finitude, alongside the sheer quantity of things there are to possibly know. The concept of faith has become a "dirty word". This is exemplified by the popularisation of "Faith Vs Reason", or "Religion Vs Science" debates, as though they are inherently dichotomous. The reality is that the discussion on faith is much more nuanced than this. Faith can be guided by reason, and reason can lead to points where a leap of faith is necessary for further progress to take place.

A great example of this can be found with the problem of the external world. During the early enlightenment period in the 16th and 17th centuries, there was a growing revival of scepticism. There are several possible reasons for this. There was the Protestant Reformation in 1517,[81] the expansion of empires abroad leading to the discovery of many new cultures,[82] and the translations of ancient Greek writers on scepticism like that of *Sextus Empiricus* published by *Henricus Stephanus*.[83] This all appears to have possibly fuelled the popularisation of scepticism enough to motivate the French philosopher *René Descartes* to want to combat it. On this, Harry Bracken says:

> "Contemporaries may have found sceptical arguments a source of fun and intellectual pleasure, but Descartes was never amused. He saw scepticism as a menace, a menace which could not be constrained within the limits of theological/religious debate."[84]

With the rise of scepticism, dogmatically held beliefs were beginning to be questioned and one by one, things people had taken for granted were beginning to be discussed. One of the subjects that began to be discussed

---

of societies based on the number of people living in better conditions. What we mean by "better conditions" is having basic material needs met (such as food, water, clothes, shelter, and so on).
81   Britannica, The Editors of Encyclopaedia. "Reformation". Encyclopedia Britannica, 2 Dec. 2022,
82   Such as the America's, the Indian Sub-Continent, The Philippines, etc.; all of which occurred leading up to the 16th century.
83   For more on "the revival of scepticism in the early modern period", see: Bican Şahin, *Toleration: The Liberal Virtue*, (Lexington Books, 2010) p. 17-20
84   Harry M. Bracken, *Descartes* (Oxford: Oneworld Publications, 2002), p. 15.

was the very existence of the external world. Most people go about their daily business and act as though it is beyond doubt that the world outside of them exists. It rarely goes questioned, and it is not likely that many people have tried to come up with sound deductive arguments which prove necessarily that the external world does in fact exist and is not the figment of someone's imagination, or an illusion created by Descartes' hypothetical evil demon.[85] It turns out that coming up with a perfectly sound deductive argument for the external world is quite difficult. You can see this difficulty being expressed through the development of ideas that begin with Descartes and continue through other philosophers like John Locke, George Berkeley, and Emmanuel Kant.

Long story short, this back and forth between the above characters eventually leads to Kant talking of the distinction between phenomena and noumena. Phenomena are the objects of our experience as presented to us by the mind and noumena are the things in themselves, which are distinct from our experiences and ultimately *unknowable*.[86] What he means to show by this is that we, as conscious beings, have access only to our experiences. Ultimately, we can never know anything about the things which give rise to our experiences. That is, we are stuck peering through the veil of our perceptions, and the "external world" is beyond our epistemic horizon and out of our reach. Our minds receive information, but they always filter it through a cognitive process before the experience is presented to us as a phenomenon. We never get pure unadulterated information. The brain is always processing it first before it presents it to us.

The reason I mention this development is because it flies in the face of the notion that everything requires an argument to be believed. I would posit, as I think most people would, that it is perfectly reasonable to go about the world and to continue living as though the external world does exist, despite not having an argument in justification of this belief. I would go further than this and argue that it is completely unreasonable to expect everyone to have an in-depth argument on such things.[87]

---

85   "I will suppose therefore that...some malicious demon of the utmost power and cunning has employed all his energies to deceive me. I shall think that the sky, the air, the earth, colours, shapes, sounds and all external things are merely the delusions of dreams which he has devised to ensnare my judgement. I shall consider myself as not having hands or eyes, or flesh, or blood or senses." - Descartes R., *The Philosophical Writings of Descartes: Volume II*, Trans. By Cottingham J., Stoothoff R., & Murdoch D., (Cambridge: Cambridge University Press, 1999). *Meditations* I, Vol.2, p. 15

86   Stang, Nicholas F., "Kant's Transcendental Idealism", *The Stanford Encyclopedia of Philosophy* (Winter 2022 Edition), Edward N. Zalta & Uri Nodelman (eds.),

87   This is not to say we can do this for absolutely any belief. There are certain

Furthermore, the scientific community move forward with this same assumption. They do not give explicit justification for the existence of an external world that is intelligible, nor do they need to. Science just works, and the approach with regards to many of the fundamental questions here ends up being a pragmatic one. We get results from it, and we reap the benefits. There is no need to waste time questioning our assumptions about this.

Finally, the kind of faith I am arguing in defence of here is not *blind faith*, but rather, *guided faith*. There are still reasons people may take a leap in one direction rather than another, but this does not negate the fact that they are still leaps. I am not making a blanket accusation against the scientific community that they all make exclusively blind leaps of faith. Nor am I saying that there are no cases of theists making blind leaps as well. All I am trying to get you to do is leave behind these childish notions that its only silly religious people that have faith and that it's something we can avoid. Admit you have it, analyse yourself and your beliefs and try to determine where your faith lies, by being open and honest about it. You own it. Only then can this discussion move forward productively.

I hope that I have shown that the dialogue surrounding the concept of faith is a nuanced one, and I hope I have convinced you not to fall into these oversimplified binaries. I will now ask you to make a leap of faith with me, not into belief, but into action.

---

criteria that can be discussed to outline what kind of beliefs could be rationally held without argument. However, this goes beyond the aim of this work. I mention it only to show the reader that faith in things comes quite naturally to the human being and can play a part in the process of reasoning for those who engage in actively mapping out and justifying their beliefs. Most of us act in the world believing it to be an existent thing without explicitly thought-out justifications, and even those who go down the path of justification inevitably have to make leaps of faith along the way.

On Finding Balance

Hopefully so far, we have paved a way towards helping people be more open to the ideas that are going to be coming up. The next step I would like to take is to offer a suggestion for a certain way of being and a brief explanation as to why this is important. First and foremost, I want to make something clear. I will not be asking the reader to take a blind leap of faith into religion. However, I will discuss the possibility of taking a leap of faith with regards to certain practices.

The reason I will be asking you to practise these things is that I believe there is a potential that it will open you up further to the possibility of theism, and more specifically, to Islam. I want to suggest to you to avoid doing certain things that I believe can cause great harm and offer nothing but mind fog and distractions to someone who is seeking truth. There are many things prohibited by the Qur'an and Sunnah, but I wish to focus on some things over others. Namely, the prohibition of alcohol, drugs, gambling, foul language, and sexual immorality. The problems that societies face because of these things are likely to be more obvious to some than others. However, I do not wish to give you a long tangent on why they are bad or how exactly they effect society, as it is beyond the scope of this book.[88] For the time being, I wish to put this forward as a personally recommended first step for a consciously made leap of faith. I hope that you will see the benefits these decisions will give you and that you experience the wisdom behind their restrictions first-hand. The main line of reasoning I will give to motivate you is that these things can consume your time and money, be addictive, and can be mentally and/or physically damaging. If you are engaging in any of them, stop. God willing you will begin to see the benefits of leaving them behind.

I will give an analogy to help you understand what it is I am attempting to do with this suggestion. Imagine you wake up in an underwater cave

---

[88] Maybe this will make for an interesting topic for a piece of writing in the future.

with scuba gear on and just enough air to get out and to the surface. The water is murky and filled with dirt and mud. You think the best course of action is to do something, and so you kick and punch your way around trying to move the dust out of the way and get some clarity. The more you try to do the worse your vision becomes, and the more dirt you kick up into the water. However, if you were to stop moving around and stayed patient for a moment, you would see that the dust would begin to settle, and the water would become a little clearer with each passing moment. If you waited long enough, the water would become clear enough for you to see through. You could begin to explore the area and find a way out. With this leap of faith, I am simply asking you to stop kicking up mud. Time is of the essence. If you can take this leap with me, you'll save yourself a lot of problems. So please, stop using intoxicants, stop gambling, stop talking in foul ways, and stop engaging in sexual immorality. Let the water settle and let your mind become clear from distractions.

> Abu Huraira reported: The Messenger of Allah, peace and blessings be upon him, said, "Verily, when the servant commits a sin, a black mark appears upon his heart. If he abandons the sin, seeks forgiveness, and repents, then his heart will be polished. If he returns to the sin, the blackness will be increased until it overcomes his heart. It is the covering that Allah has mentioned: No, rather a covering is over their hearts from what they have earned." (83:14)[89]

As the Hadith suggests, the bad habits that you are engaging in can be an impediment to your vision. When we engage in addictive behaviour, we can become so focused on the objects of our desires that it becomes difficult to see or focus on other things. Make a pledge to give them up and allow the benefits of this to manifest themselves to you.

This is not a necessary step, as I am sure people can and do still find guidance despite engaging forbidden acts regularly. It is also the case that when the heart and mind settle on belief in Islam that a heavy sense of duty can overcome the believer, motivating them to give up the bad; being a common consequence of this.

In any case, there is certainly wisdom in following such prohibitions, and taking up the opportunity to gain an insight through direct experience of its benefits. I think this will be something that could potentially help you incline towards the right direction. If you are patient and stick with it through the initial difficulty of leaving behind addictive behaviour, I am sure this wisdom could become apparent, removing yet another obstacle between you and belief in Islam.

---

[89] Sunan al-Tirmidhi 3334,

Another thing I would recommend is prostrating to your Creator and asking Him for guidance. If you are open to the idea, a moment of sincere openness while pleading with Him to guide you to the truth can have a profound effect. I know many people who have embraced Islam who can pinpoint having done this at some point in their journey (including myself). Being open to the possibility of His existence and attempting to develop a relationship with Him is a way in which you can draw closer to Him and His religion.

PART 4

Islam as an Antidote

The Final Step

The next step is to give an explication of why Islam can help to stem both the causes and the effects of nihilism, I have mentioned so far. It is beyond the purpose of this book to prove Islam explicitly, and I would like to refer you to a few works that I believe will help with this goal in the footnotes.[90] If God wills, I do intend to give a systematic overview of these proofs myself in more detail in the future, but not now. This will be a large project, so I will put it to the side for the time being to focus on the issue of nihilism in relation to Islam and how Islam deals with the problems that I have been outlining. What will follow will be a step-by-step overview of each of the problems previously mentioned that either cause nihilism and how Islam prevents them, or with regards to the consequences of nihilism and how Islam resolves them.

---

90   A translation of the Qur'an you can understand, The Divine Reality by Hamza Tzortzis, The Eternal Challenge and Forbidden prophecies both by Abu Zakiriyya. (Check bibliography for full references)

Recommending Prevention and Cure

Friedrich Nietzsche is the most famous name associated with ideas concerning nihilism. He is most famous for declaring the "death of God", and thus the onset of nihilism upon the society that he brazenly declares to have "killed" Him. It is important to stress here that Nietzsche did not mean this in a literal sense. Rather, he was simply referring to the fact that in western society, a particular historical movement had taken place that saw them slowly but surely throwing the prevailing religion out of the window. They were losing faith in Christianity because the higher values it promoted were undermining the foundations of Christianity. He did not think highly of this religion at all, and one of his final works was intended to be an all-out assault on it; aptly named "The Anti-Christ: A Criticism of Christianity". Yet in this very book – often associated with a general "anti-religious" agenda and his final work before he stopped writing altogether – Nietzsche had some very interesting things to say about Islam. In aphorism 60, he says the following:

> Christianity destroyed the harvest we might have reaped from the culture of antiquity, later it also destroyed our harvest of the culture of Islam. The wonderful Moorish world of Spanish culture, which in its essence is more closely related to us, and which appeals more to our sense and taste than Rome and Greece, was trampled to death (I do not say by what kind of feet), why? Because it owed its origin to noble, to manly instincts, because it said yea to life, even that life so full of the rare and refined luxuries of the Moors! . . . Later on, the Crusaders waged war upon something before which it would have been more seemly in them to grovel in the dust, a culture, beside which even our Nineteenth Century would seem very poor and very "senile." Of course they wanted the booty: the Orient was rich. . . . For goodness' sake let us forget our prejudices! Crusades—superior piracy, that is all! German nobility—that is to say, a Viking nobility at bottom, was in its element in such wars:

> the Church was only too well aware of how German nobility is to be won. . . . German nobility was always the "Swiss Guard" of the Church, always at the service of all the bad instincts of the Church; but it was well paid for it all. . . . Fancy the Church having waged its deadly war upon everything noble on earth, precisely with the help of German swords, German blood, and courage! A host of painful questions might be raised on this point. German nobility scarcely takes a place in the history o higher culture: the reason of this is obvious Christianity, alcohol—the two great means of corruption. As a matter of fact, choice ought to be just as much out of the question between Islam and Christianity, as between an Arab and a Jew. The decision is already self-evident; nobody is at liberty to exercise a choice in this matter. A man is either of the Chandala or he is not. . . . "War with Rome to the knife! Peace and friendship with Islam": this is what that great free spirit, that genius among German emperors, Frederick the Second, not only felt but also did. What? Must a German in the first place be a genius, a free-spirit, in order to have decent feelings? I cannot understand how a German was ever able to have Christian feelings.[91]

This is quite obviously a very intriguing passage, especially considering how often Nietzsche is put forward as one of the forefathers of the atheistic movement. Yet despite this, he held Islam in high regard. Now I'm by no means going to suggest that he would be completely for all Islamic values, as there may be some overlap concerning his critiques of Christianity to Islam. I do not wish to deny that and do not promote his views wholesale. Despite his criticisms however, he referred to Islam as "noble" and praised it for its "manly" instincts. Although there may be some overlap between Christianity and Islam, there is a great deal that makes the two religions distinct, and it is this distinction that seems to be what sets Islam aside as something admirable for Nietzsche. He even goes as far as expressing his desire that Germany had embraced Islam rather than Christianity. This begs the question: did Nietzsche also see something in Islam that meant it could be utilised as an antidote to the sickness of nihilism? There is no doubt that this question will demand some very nuanced answers, as he is by no means a clear-cut Muslim. However, I hope to convince the reader that, regardless of what Nietzsche thought in the end, Islam *can* be that antidote!

---

91   Nietzsche F., *The Anti-Christ: A Criticism of Christianity,* trans. By A.M. Ludovici, (New York; Barnes & Noble, 2006), p.72

So let us begin now by showing how Islam will tackle the causes of nihilism, which in turn will show how Islam will prevent it from continuing to manifest as a societal issue and help to install meaning and purpose in the lives of those who submit to their Creator and the religion He has provided for them. It will also simultaneously cover how Islam will deal with the effects of nihilism that are present in a society already caught in the grips of such a malady. There is an overlap between the two, and the same references and points I make for the preventative measures will also be things that can be used to heal the sickness that is already present. If I can show how Islam deals with these issues, then we have the tools for which we can remedy many of the problems that face society today.

Post-Truth and Epistemic Nihilism

In Islam, there is a strong emphasis on upholding the truth and that it is, in fact, something attainable. In the Qur'an, Allah states:

> And declare, "The truth has come, and falsehood has vanished. Indeed, falsehood is bound to vanish."[92]

There is no "post-truth" in Islam. Facts cannot be picked and chosen based on whims. The believer is also commanded to uphold the truth and be honest in his affairs. To stand for justice, even if it be against himself or those he loves.[93] Allah, The Lord of all the Worlds, is Al-Alim (The All-Knowing) and He is Al-Haqq (the Truth). There is an emphasis on the fact that we cannot hide anything from Him, that He knows what we hide within ourselves[94] and that not even a leaf can fall without His knowing it.[95] Simply put, there are facts about us and about the world. Islam establishes this and gives the believer no reason to doubt it, and it demands from us that we concern ourselves to the best of our abilities with truth. We are to turn to Allah and acknowledge to ourselves that it is fruitless to conceal the truth; and we should make repentance for our misdeeds. We are not to conceal the truth, and nor are we to lie, or to try and cover it up.

With regards to our prophet ﷺ, there is a Hadith that states that "whoever tells a lie against me (the prophet), then let him occupy his seat in Hellfire."[96] It is quotes like these and many others that have motivated a severe concern with the etiquettes surrounding establishing the truth to the best of our abilities and has consistently been a huge part of the Islamic tradition.

Truth exists, Allah knows it, and we will be held accountable for our lack of concern with attaining it. As Islam commands the truth, affirms its

---

92   Quran, 17:81
93   Ibid., 4:135
94   Ibid., 11:5
95   Ibid., 6:59
96   Sahih al-Bukhari 107,

existence, and holds the believer accountable in relation to it, those who become believers are given a shield against the notion of "epistemic nihilism". That is, insofar as you are a Muslim, you cannot claim that truth is not attainable, when Allah Himself gives you the Truth, and commands you to uphold it. To go against this would be to rebel against Allah and His words.

To show a great example of this point, we have a hadith narrated by Ibn `Abbas which displays exactly what I've been saying. Truth exists, and you cannot hide it from Him who knows everything:

> Whenever the Prophet (ﷺ) offered the night prayer, he used to say, «O Allah! All Praise is for You; You are the Light of the Heavens and the Earth. And all Praise is for You; You are the Keeper of the Heavens and the Earth. All Praise is for You; You are the Lord of the Heavens and the Earth and whatever is therein. You are the Truth, and Your Promise is the Truth, and Your Speech is the Truth, and meeting You is the Truth, and Paradise is the Truth and Hell (Fire) is the Truth and all the prophets are the Truth and the Hour is the Truth. O Allah! I surrender to You, and believe in You, and depend upon You, and repent to You, and in Your cause I fight and with Your orders I rule. So please forgive my past and future sins and those sins which I did in secret or in public. It is You Whom I worship, None has the right to be worshipped except You.» [97]

We also have another one narrated by the companion Abdullah who reported what Allah›s Messenger ﷺ said about the importance of truth and upholding it:

> **It is obligatory for you to tell the truth,** for truth leads to virtue and virtue leads to Paradise, and the man who continues to speak the truth and endeavours to tell the truth is eventually recorded as truthful with Allah, and beware of telling of a lie for telling of a lie leads to obscenity and obscenity leads to Hell-Fire, and the person who keeps telling lies and endeavours to tell a lie is recorded as a liar with Allah.[98]

You cannot simultaneously be a Muslim and an epistemic nihilist. We may be limited, and prone to making mistakes, but we do our best to be sincere and honest, and to express the facts to the highest degree of our ability. We

---

97 Sahih al-Bukhari 7499,
98 Sahih Muslim 2607c,

recognise that declaring truth and knowledge inaccessible is to ultimately make a truth and a knowledge claim. To utter such a statement is to declare that very statement as a piece of knowledge which can be known to be true. We declare negating the possibility of truth and knowledge as absurd and use our rational faculties to incline to truth wherever we find it.

In another narration, another of the companions, Abu Huraira, reported:

> The Messenger of Allah, peace and blessings be upon him, said, **"Whoever takes a path upon which to obtain knowledge, Allah makes the path to Paradise easy for him."**[99]

So go, reader, seek truth and knowledge and take it as your own!

---

[99] Jami' at-Tirmidhi 2646,

Overcoming Pessimism & Instilling Hope

Pessimism is completely impermissible in Islam. We are to be, in a sense, *tragic optimists*. We understand that life can be difficult. We understand that sometimes things get hard, and it can be challenging to deal with. Many times, in life you may feel that you are pushed to your very limits. But Allah tells us that He "does not burden a soul with more than it can bear".[100] We have also been promised by Allah that we will be tested, and so we should not let our guard down and prepare ourselves with the necessary qualities that will help us succeed. Allah says many things in the Qur'an to this effect, to keep us mindful of the tragedies that befall us in life. Here are a few more examples of verses in the Qur'an that express this point:

1. "Do people think once they say, "We believe," that they will be left without being put to the test? We have certainly tested those before them. And (in this way) Allah will clearly distinguish between those who are truthful and those who are liars."[101]

2. "We will certainly test you (believers) until We prove those of you who (truly) struggle (in Allah's cause) and remain steadfast and reveal how you conduct yourselves."[102]

3. "Do you think you will be admitted into Paradise without being tested like those before you? They were afflicted with suffering and adversity and were so (violently) shaken that (even) the Messenger and the believers with him cried out, "When will Allah's help come?" Indeed, Allah's help is (always) near."[103]

---

100 Qur'an, 2:286
101 Ibid., 29:2-3
102 Ibid., 47:31
103 Ibid., 2:214

> 4. "Every soul will taste death. And We test you (O humanity) with good and evil as a trail, then to Us you will (all) be returned."[104]

Life is most certainly going to get difficult; we know this, and the Qur'an acknowledges that. Many of us, if God wills, will grow elderly, and will inevitably have to deal with the ailments that come along with old age. We will suffer illness, stress, anxiety, and fear. We will deal with loss, of loved ones and of property. Everything in this world turns to dust. We are tested so that we can show who we truly are. As it is only when things become difficult that our convictions will be made apparent. It is easy to show "strength" when nothing is hard. It is easy to be "brave" when there is no danger. We see this on social media all the time. From behind the safety of a screen people abuse others in a way they would never do in person. They are safe behind the screen and so act "strong" or "confident", but if they found themselves face to face with the same person in real life, they may quickly turn out to be weak cowards. How can you truly praise someone as brave if they have not had the opportunity to prove it? And how can you say that someone is steadfast upon their religion if not faced with difficulty and hardship?

This life is a test filled with difficulties, but this is not something that should make us lose hope! In fact, according to Islam everything the believer suffers is good for him.

> Abu Huraira reported: The Prophet, peace and blessings be upon him, said: "Nothing afflicts a Muslim of hardship, nor illness, nor anxiety, nor sorrow, nor harm, nor distress, nor even the pricking of a thorn, but that Allah will expiate his sins by it."[105]

In this hadith, it is made very clear that any discomfort of any kind is a means by which we relieve ourselves of a burden on Judgement Day. We are given promises of paradise in the Qur'an and told that our sins can be an obstacle to obtaining it. However, suffering here is completely transformed from a negative experience to a positive one, in that you know it is for a greater good, and that ultimately you benefit from going through hardship.

> Mus'ab bin Sa'd narrated from his father that a man said: "O Messenger of Allah! Which of the people is tried most severely?" He said: "The Prophets, then those nearest to them, then those nearest to them. A man is tried according to his religion; if he is firm in his religion, then his trials are more severe, and if he is

---

104 Ibid., 21:35
105 Sahih al-Bukhari 5641,

frail in his religion, then he is tried according to the strength of his religion. The servant shall continue to be tried until he is left walking upon the earth without any sins."[106]

It may seem strange to someone who does not have faith, but the believer is all too familiar with the bittersweetness they experience in hardship. Yes, it is difficult for them. But when they know their religion, it can be easy for them to be thankful to Allah, and they praise him by saying "Alhamdulillah" despite their hardships. The pain still hurts, but there is sweetness to it because of this knowledge. This sweetness instils hope and makes it difficult to be a pessimist when you think that everything happens for a good and wise purpose.

> Suhayb reported: The Messenger of Allah, peace and blessings be upon him, said "Wondrous is the affair of a believer, as there is good for him in every matter; this is not the case for anyone but a believer. If he experiences pleasure, he thanks Allah, and it is good for him. If he experiences harm, he shows patience, and it is good for him."[107]

Everything is good for the believer. Nothing befalls him but that it increases his love for his Maker. When He knows Allah and His attributes, he knows that his Creator is Wise and Merciful. He knows that Allah is Loving. He knows that his Lord would not deprive him of goodness:

> Abu Razin reported: The Messenger of Allah, peace and blessing be upon him, said, "Allah laughs for the despair of His servant, as He will soon relieve him." I said, "O messenger of Allah, does the Lord laugh?" The Prophet said, "Yes." I said, "We will never be deprived of goodness by a Lord who laughs!"[108]

How can you fall into pessimism knowing and believing in all of this? Just with these Hadith alone, we have enough to show that those who believes in Islam, has all they need to defend themselves against pessimistic tendencies towards life and the hardship they may face therein. We may suffer, but it is a means by which we may be filled with joy on The Day of Judgement. We can look forward to a day that the things we regret doing will be taken away because we were patient in adversity. We can look forward to being honoured because of our striving and being strong and steadfast for the

---

106   Jami' at-Tirmidhi 2398,
107   Sahih Muslim 2999,
108   Sunan Ibn Majah 181,

sake of Allah. I, as a believer, read these statements and it makes my heart sore with hope.

Allah tells us that on "the Day He will gather them; it will be as if they had not stayed (in the world) except for an hour of a day...".[109] Our perception of the life we lived will feel as though it was short – a fleeting moment – and the pleasure of what awaits us will be enough to make us forget every pain we have ever experienced, as stated in the following Hadith:

> And then one of the people of Jannah who had experienced extreme misery in the life of this world will be dipped in Jannah. Then he will be asked: ‹O son of Adam! Did you ever experience any misery? Did you ever encounter difficulty?› He will say: «By Allah, no my Rabb, I neither experienced misery nor passed through hardship».[110]

This is not completely inconceivable. In fact, we have practical examples of this in this world, without even having to refer to the next life. For example, when I was a young boy at the age of 1, I fell down some stairs with a plate that smashed and cut my face open. I nearly bled to death on the floor. Thankfully, I was taken to the hospital, and they managed to stitch my face; I recovered, all praise be to God. I can imagine this experience and the recovery period afterwards included a lot of pain. However, I have no memory of it. I do not recall the experience at all. I only know what my mother has told me about it, and from the pictures I have seen.

There have been other events that have caused me great pain in life, and if I think back on them, I can recall the pain, but not as severely as it was experienced at the time. I can remember it hurt, but not with the same intensity. It is like looking back into fog as I can barely make out the experience.

When I was younger, I had dreams which terrified me. I dreamt of horrible things occurring to me that have put me in an intense state of fear and panic. Upon waking up however, I would quickly move on from the ordeal and continue to live my life as if nothing had happened. I have family members and friends who have suffered even greater ordeals, but you would not think they had suffered at all if you met and spoke with them. Especially with how strong and as stable as they appear in the present day, and how they can laugh and smile despite what they had been through.

Furthermore, upon experiencing something pleasurable in this life – something amazing – we quickly forget whatever suffering we may have

---

109   Qur'an 10:45
110   Riyad as-Salihin 461,

gone through in the past. We can quickly forget *everything*! For example, as a non-Muslim I used to frequent the Casino and would often see old men wonder in with what looked like every ailment under the sun, hunched over and recoiling in discomfort. But if they won a significant amount of money, they would soon look fit as a fiddle, jumping around with joy at their "victory" against the casino. It was as if they had not suffered at all. If this is so with the meagre pleasures of this world, consider what could possibly be forgotten upon receiving the pleasures of Paradise which are described to be completely overwhelming and unimaginable:

> Abu Huraira reported: The Prophet, peace and blessings be upon him, said, "Allah said, "I have prepared for My righteous slaves (such excellent things) as no eye has ever seen, nor any ear has ever heard, nor a human heart can ever conceive."[111]

How can anyone despair and become pessimistic with such promises? If Islam is truly accepted and embodied by a person, they have with themselves all they need as a shield against the woes of pessimism. And if pessimism is a necessary precursor to nihilism, then it follows they have a shield against that as well.

---

[111] Sahih al-Bukhari 7498,

Combatting Scepticism and Moral Nihilism

First, we must understand that scepticism in and of itself is not necessarily a bad thing. It is required to even consider being a Muslim in the first place. There is a lot of misinformation being shared on Islam that you need to apply a certain level of scepticism, to sift through the nonsense and obtain the truth. Not being sceptical at all with regards to this information would be the cause of someone never taking Islam seriously as a potential option. For example, one of the main claims levied against Islam is that it requires you not to use your intellect and have unquestioning blind faith in the religion. It is also claimed that it offers you no reason beyond threats of violence to accept it. However, if you read the Qur'an, you find the very opposite. We have explicit verses that implore the reader to use their reason: "Thus does Allah makes clear to you His verses so that you might use reason."[112] Or the disbelievers regretting not using their reason when it is too late: "And they will lament, "If only we had listened and reasoned, we would not be among the residents of the Blaze!""[113]

Furthermore, we have the story of Abraham, peace be upon him. He is a main figurehead within the Islamic tradition. In chapter 21 of the Qur'an, we have the story of him engaging with his people who were idol worshippers and imploring them to think logically about what they were doing. He rebukes them for failing to use their reason saying:

> "Do you then worship – instead of Allah – What can neither benefit nor harm you in any way? Shame on you and whatever you worship instead of Allah! Do you not use reason?"[114]

---

112   Qur'an 2:242
113   Ibid., 67:10
114   Ibid., 21:66-67

We can see here that the proper use of reason is not at all rejected by the Islamic tradition, but quite the opposite. It is commanded! Those who fail to use it do a disservice to themselves and their community. This critique of blind following doesn't stop with Abraham and his people either. The same critique was levied against the Quraysh:

> "When it is said to them, "Follow what Allah has revealed," they reply, "No! We (only) follow what we found our forefathers practicing." (Would they still do so) even if Satan is inviting them to the torment of the Blaze?"[115]

This mentality is something that never fully seems to go away, as it is something I must deal with even today. It was only very recently I got into a discussion about religion on the bus with a Christian, who upon finding out I was a Muslim told me I should follow the religion of "my people" and that Islam was a religion for the Arabs. It seems that he had forgotten that Jesus was an Arab (and I made sure to remind him of this).

Furthermore, it is also important to mention that we must recognise the limits of reason and that it can only ever take us so far. For example, let us say that you live in a terrace house, and I live next door to you. You can deduce I exist from certain evidence, but you can only know so much about me with reason alone. You may know that I have guests over at certain times because you can hear us talking through our thin walls; you may know I'm a Muslim because I play the Qur'an loudly from time to time, or that I like watching loud action movies in the evening; you may also know that I like to eat certain foods because I have it delivered, and so on. All these things can be deduced as reasonable inferences, but it is only going to get you so far. Watching a person will only tell you so much about them or the house in which they live if you do not have first-hand experience of it, or if they do not tell you that information.

The limits of reason can be shown to occur within creation, and this limit, by greater reason, can also be extended to discussions about God. We can make certain inferences based on evidence and deductions that there must be a necessary being that is alive and has a will, that must be powerful, wise, and knowledgeable etc.[116] But if we want to know more about this being, we can only get that information through communication with it.

---

115 Ibid., 31:21
116 For more details on this see The Divine Reality and The Londoniyya, (both available through Sapience Institute). Also, episodes on the Thought Adventure Podcast. I will also be releasing a more detailed explanation of these steps in the future God willing.

This is where the need for revelation comes in and the human being is reduced to conjecture without being given explicit information from a trustworthy source. If we have good reasons to believe a God exists and have good reasons to believe Islam is the accepted religion of this God, then we have good reasons to accept what God tells us about Himself. So, when He explains to us that He is Al-Ghaffar (The Great Forgiver), for example, we can accept this as an inference that has its foundation in a reliable scripture that comes from Him. We can also only know about the events that will occur on Judgement Day, or the contents of heaven, if He tells us about them. Just as you will not know anything about how my house is set up and what is in there if you have not seen the inside of my home or been told about the contents, and then try to use reason alone to work it out. Reason in and off itself – without direct experience or trustworthy testimony – is not going to be of any assistance in getting answers to these questions.

With regards to these secondary things that we take from scripture, so long as there is no direct presence of something like an explicit contradiction, we have no reason to be sceptical of them to the degree that we reject them completely. Their truth is dependent on whether God exists, and whether The Qur'an is from Him. If the answer to these questions is yes, then we can accept what comes from them. Just as if you do not have access to my house, or more information about me, you can only really go by what you get from myself as testimony, or someone else who has that knowledge that you trust. Furthermore, to reject these secondary claims as the consequence of your scepticism also showcases a lack of scepticism in other domains of thought. For example, if someone rejects claims of miracles as the result of scepticism, then what they are doing is holding that common experience should not have scepticism applied to it. A true sceptic may potentially hold such claims at arm's length, but they wouldn't dismiss them outright because we can also apply scepticism to our own experiences and ask whether we can say we that we in fact *truly know* that miracles are impossible.

For someone who becomes a believer, an avenue for developing a relationship with The Creator is opened. With this occurring, you can learn about the names and attributes of Allah as revealed in the Qur'an (Allah's words) and the Sunnah (knowledge from the Prophet ﷺ). In this, we find that Allah reveals to us that He is Al-Haqq (The Absolute Truth), Al- 'Aleem (The All Knowing), Al-Hakeem (The Most Wise), Al-Barr (The Source of Goodness), Al-Haadi (The Guide), and Al-Hakam (The Giver of Justice), among many others. If it is established that Islam is true, then we can understand *who* Allah is in His nature and implement this understanding into our daily lives with everything we come to face, be it good or bad.

As it is stated in the Qur'an: "We have no knowledge except what You have taught us. You are truly the All-Knowing, All-Wise."[117] Which is to say, Allah has the best perspective, which is full and comprehensive, missing nothing. We are finite and always suffer from ignorance in many things when engaging in the pursuit of knowledge. The things we know are snapshots into an incomprehensibly large universe. Many of the propositions we put forward, be that in science or philosophy, are underpinned by a great many assumptions about reality and ourselves. However, Allah does not suffer from ignorance as we do, and so if there is any true knowledge to be attained, it would be that which is given to us by such a being.

> "With Him are the keys of the unseen—no one knows them except Him. And He knows what is in the land and sea. Not even a leaf falls without His knowledge, nor a grain in the darkness of the earth or anything—green or dry—but is [written] in a perfect Record."[118]

Nothing escapes The One who creates and sustains everything, always, and so it would be fruitless to argue with Him. Just as it would be fruitless for a young child to argue with their parents over whether they should be allowed to only eat ice cream and nothing else. However, it must be stressed that the analogy here does not give justice to the difference in knowledge between God and creation. The difference between Allah's knowledge and our own is unquantifiable, especially compared to the difference between the parent and the child. My mentioning this is only to elicit an insight into the nature of when the ignorant may still wish to argue with someone more knowledgeable. This argumentative reaction happens precisely because of their ignorance and their inability to reflect on their own limitations and to transcend beyond their own desires for quick pleasures and gratification.

Now, what about morality? If you have accepted Allah as your Lord, and Muhammad ﷺ as your messenger, can you really say there are no moral truths to be found? Or more specifically, that moral discourse is itself somehow flawed and prone to error like that of the "phlogiston" discourse?[119]

---

117 Qur'an, 2:32
118 Ibid., 6:59
119 A superseded scientific theory that at one point in time was held by the scientific community during the 1600's. They once believed there to be a fire-like substance which was released by combustible bodies when they were on fire. They had a whole discourse on this, and the intelligentsia would talk back and forth regarding their evidence for something which later was found to be false. The comparison to morality here is that the moral nihilist claims that moral discourse

Islam offers a solution to this because of the guidance given to us in the Qur'an and Sunnah. Muhammad ﷺ is said to be a walking Qur'an. He is a means by which we can come to understand the etiquette of a believer and an example to follow, as expressed in the following Hadith:

> Jabir ibn Abdullah reported: The Messenger of Allah, peace and blessings be upon him, said, "Verily, Allah has sent me with the perfection of noble morals and completion of good deeds."[120]

Furthermore, the Qur'an itself makes it very clear that what we are being given by Allah is the criterion to be able to practically apply moral judgements and determine what we ought and ought not to do:

> "[…] the Quran was revealed as guidance for mankind, clear messages giving guidance and distinguishing between right and wrong."[121]

Without a firm rope to grasp onto, mankind is left to float in the abyss without knowledge. We quickly and easily become lost, arguing amongst each other endlessly over mere speculations about how we ought to behave. The secular western world continually moves the lines that distinguish good from evil. In line with this, they establish numerous insufficient moral philosophies to fill the void left by the loss of faith in religious traditions. This continual bickering has led to the alienation and isolation of many people within modern society. It is this, along with a heavy leaning towards the related philosophies, that pushes naive ideas of freedom and individuality and contributes to the increased fracturing of our increasingly diverse societies. However, with Islam, we are offered an opportunity to unite. As Allah says in the Quran:

> And hold firmly to the rope of Allah and do not be divided. Remember Allah's favour upon you when you were enemies, then He united your hearts, so you—by His grace—became brothers. And you were at the brink of a fiery pit, and He saved you from it. This is how Allah makes His revelations clear to you, so that you may be [rightly] guided.[122]

---

is akin to phlogiston discourse. They believe it is ultimately false and not a discussion about anything that has any reality. Another name for this position is "error theory" because it believes the discourse to be based on an "error".

120   Al-Mu'jam al-Awsat 7073,
121   Qur'an, 2:185
122   ibid, 3:103

Islam offers the guidance that people are yearning for because of the void left with the loss of religion and tradition in the modern world. It gives people something to orient themselves with and to gain a common direction; a centre point to circumnavigate with each other. Furthermore, in line with the above quote from the Qur'an, a common note that people make when going on a pilgrimage to Mecca is how unified the people become when united upon the religion of Islam. It effectively offers a practical solution to the fracturing of society I have mentioned. Malcom X makes a beautiful description of his experience during hajj, and how he saw that it effectively eradicated things like racial and class tensions that he was very familiar with in the United States (a problem that is still present today in many parts of the world). In The New York Times they wrote that he says the following:

> During the past seven days of this holy pilgrimage, while undergoing the rituals of the hajj [pilgrimage], I have eaten from the same plate, drank from the same glass, slept on the same bed or rug, while praying to the same God—not only with some of this earth's most powerful kings, cabinet members, potentates and other forms of political and religious rulers —but also with fellow-Muslims whose skin was the whitest of white, whose eyes were the bluest of blue, and whose hair was the blondest of blond—yet it was the first time in my life that I didn't see them as 'white' men. I could look into their faces and see that these people didn't regard themselves as 'white.' Their belief in the Oneness of God (Allah) had actually removed the 'white' from their minds, which automatically changed their attitude and behaviour toward people of other colours. Their belief in the Oneness of God has actually made them so different from American whites, their outer physical characteristics played no part at all in my mind during all my close associations with them.[123]

Islam is a solution to many of the moral and ethical issues we face as a society and more specifically, a solution to *nihilism*. We do not need to suffer the ailments we currently face under a world governed mostly by worldly pursuits that can never be fully satisfied, driven by unrestricted materialism and hedonistic desires. The doors to this solution remain firmly open. Just as Islam was able to completely change an apparently insignificant and troubled society that lived in the middle of nowhere, into a flourishing and successful people that have reached every corner of the globe, it can also

---

123   Malcolm X, 'Malcolm X Pleased by Whites' Attitude On Trip to Mecca', *The New York* Times, 8 May 1964,

transform us. All it takes is for you, the reader, to take the step of seeing Islam for what it is: as a serious alternative to the current destructive path we walk on together across the globe.

Patience, Contentment & Perseverance

Islam puts an incredibly high importance on the virtue of patience and gives many good reasons to desire practising it and perfecting it within us. Within the Qur'an and sunnah, we have many stories which we can use to come to understand the importance of these virtues. One is with the story of Musa, peace be upon him, who joins a wise man named Khidr in chapter 18 (Surah Al-Kahf). This chapter is one which we are encouraged to read once a week, every Friday. It is here we read Musa requesting permission to follow the wise man so that he may learn right guidance from him. In response, Khidr says to him: "You certainly cannot be patient (enough) with me. And how can you be patient with what is beyond your (realm of) knowledge".[124]

From this story we learn that being patient can be difficult, even when it comes to the prophets, as from the verses 69 through to 82 tell of the story of Musa becoming forgetful not just once, but three times. In the end, Khidr gives the explanations of why he did what he did, which at the face of it seemed unjust or wrong to do. Musa at one point even confidently intervenes and goes as far as saying "You have certainly done a horrible thing".[125] However, he does this only to be reminded again that he was told that he could not be patient. In the end, the explanations are given, and it is said "This is the explanation of what you could not bear patiently." What is revealed shows to Musa that there is always a bigger picture to Allah's plan, for which human beings are only granted limited insight.

What we can take from this is that even the prophets, who are the greatest among the creation, in certain circumstances found it difficult to be patient. However, they were persistent in realigning themselves and always affirmed the importance of patience. With the Prophet Musa especially, we

---
124 Quran 18:67-68
125 Ibid., 18:74

know he was tested numerous times, by both his own people (when they made an idol of a calf out of their jewellery),[126] and by pharaoh on many occasions (only to be told he was bewitched).[127] Yet despite these numerous trials, Moses pushed on with his God given mission.

In conjunction with this, we have the story of Yusuf, peace be upon him, who is unjustly prisoned for crimes he did not commit. He remained there for many years as the result a fellow prisoner, who was meant to mention him to the king but forget to do so.[128] Despite this, we never hear of Yusuf complaining. He is only described as being one of the good doers, on whom Allah's mercy is showered upon, and that he is faithful and mindful of Allah.[129] The reason he can be patient is because he knows who Allah is! He knows Allah is The All-Wise, The Just and The Best of Planners. He knows that whatever is occurring in his life is exactly what is best for him, and that Allah has a grand plan to which he fits in. Allah elevates him in this world and in the next for his patience, and he is among those who are honoured as a result.

Now it is important to note that this patience can be justified within the Islamic paradigm even if things were not to be resolved in this life. Even if Yusuf, or anyone for that matter, were to end up in prison because of the injustice of someone else, and remain there until death, this would still be understood in relation to Allah as what is good for the believer. We have several narrations from the prophet Muhammad ﷺ to this effect which I have already mentioned above about everything that befalls a believer relieves him of sins,[130] and everything being good for, whether it's a blessing or a difficulty.[131]

As a Muslim, I find this to be incredibly empowering. I have within the religion, tools that can be used to turn every situation, no matter how dire, into a good one. Whatever befalls me is giving me benefit. The more difficult the trial and the more patience is required to overcome it, the more I receive in the hereafter; the more burdens I am relieved of on The Day of Judgement. We know this because we have accounts of Sahaba who were tortured, in some cases to death, by the Quraysh. Most notably, Abu Jahl – one of the cruellest in his opposition to the Muslims.

> Among the most relentless of the persecutors was Abu Jahl. If a convert had a powerful family to defend him, Abu Jahl would

---

126   Ibid., 7:148
127   Ibid., 17:101
128   Ibid., 12:42
129   Ibid., 12:56-57
130   S Sahih al-Bukhari 5641,
131   Sahih Muslim 2999,

merely insult him and promise to ruin his reputation and make him a laughingstock. If he were a merchant, he would threaten to stop his trade by organising a general boycott of his goods so that he would be ruined. If he were weak and unprotected and of his own clan, he would have him tortured: and he had powerful allies in many other clans whom he could persuade to do the same with their own weak and unprotected converts.

It was through him that his clansmen tortured three of their poorer confederates, Yasir and Sumayyah and their son 'Ammar. They refused to renounce Islam, and Sumayyah died under the sufferings they inflicted on her. [132]

These companions are an amazing example of how the teachings of Islam, when they are fully absorbed into the heart, give the believer the ability to withstand severe torture. Their faith was so high that they were more willing to be martyred than to give up on their religion. They had true certainty, and that gave them courage in the face of things that many of us would quiver to even think about it happening to us. Constantly engaging in worship and learning about who your Lord is, develops a closeness to Him that grants the believer complete submission to the plan of The Creator. You come to understand that He is The All-Knowing, He is The All-Wise, and as the repeatedly mentioned hadith reiterates, *everything is good for the believer*.[133]

The Qur'an also claims that we can "seek comfort in patience and prayer." And that "Allah is truly with those who are patient."[134] It also gives us the tools we need to develop such qualities in ourselves with constant reminders of what we may achieve in both this world and in the next if we submit to the will of God. That is, we must truly come to fully understand that many things are simply not in our control. A great source of pain for many people is caused by stressing over things they cannot do anything about. Islam pushes this out of you. Life is a test. And Allah reminds us that He "will certainly test you with a touch of fear and famine and loss of property, life, and crops." But despite all of this, He bolsters the point by adding that we should "give good news to those who patiently endure — who, when faced with a disaster, say, "Surely to Allah we belong and to Him we will [all] return.""[135]

---

132   Lings M., *Muhammad: his life based on the earliest sources*, (Cambridge: The Islamic Text Society, 2017), pp. 79-80.
133   Sahih Muslim 2999,
134   Qur'an, 2:153
135   Ibid., 2:155-156

We are given a whole month once a year to practise patience in the form of fasting. This is why the month of Ramadhan is also sometimes referred to as "The Month of Patience". A month where we do without water or food from dawn till dusk. As a Muslim, we are given many opportunities like this to develop our ability to persevere through difficulties and find contentment in the apparent chaos of life. No matter what hits us, we know that Allah is with us, and that we are a small part of the plan of The Most Wise, The Best of Planners.

Duty & Responsibility

Islam is a complete way of life, and there are set duties incumbent upon the believer which bind them to their brothers and sisters in Islam, and to humanity more generally. This is outlined in several responsibilities that each believer has towards everyone that they have around them. First and foremost, you have your duty towards God. You must worship Him at set points throughout the day, giving you structure, and helping you to develop that relationship with Him. Each prayer is an opportunity to seek forgiveness for whatever mistakes you have made and to reflect on your blessings. It functions to remind you constantly of your place in the world and that you have a duty to enjoin the good and forbid the evil. All of this contributes to a greater sense of purpose and meaning. You can come to understand with reflection upon the Qur'an that we have not been created as playthings, as Allah says: "Did you then think that We had created you without purpose, and that you would never be returned to us?"[136] But rather, we were created to be tested: "He is the One Who created death and life in order to test which of you is best in deeds"[137] And that we were created for worship: "I did not create jinn and humans except to worship me."[138] Accepting Islam binds us to this duty and pushes us to be God conscious. How can we feel a sense of meaninglessness when such a grand honour has been bestowed upon us?

On top of this, the Qur'an and Sunnah repeatedly emphasise your duty towards your parents:

> "For your Lord has decreed that you worship none but Him. And honour your parents. If one or both of them reach old age in your care, never say to them [even] 'ugh,' nor yell at them. Rather, address them respectfully. And be humble with them out of mercy,

---
[136] Ibid., 23:115
[137] Ibid., 67:2
[138] Ibid., 51:56

and pray, "My Lord! Be merciful to them as they raised me when I was young."[139]

This contrasts with the growing phenomena of parents being disrespected and rebellion against them that you see rising in modernity. Along with the growing trends of putting parents into nursing homes. In the west, things like individual autonomy and liberty are highly valued, and so anything that impedes on these values is often seen as negative. Looking after your parents in their old age can be considered a burden because it requires sacrifice. It is a difficult job, requiring a lot of effort and energy, seen as taking away from your valuable time which you could be spending on yourself.

However, we must ask ourselves what kind of world do we want to see develop? This isn't just about our parents; it is also about us. They may be the ones who are old now, but we too will one day grow old and so will our children. It is important to instil community values in the populous to help prevent many problems that arise from the neglect of such things. For example, in England more than 2 million people live alone and more than 1 million report not having contact with anyone for over a month.[140] This is unacceptable. Loneliness and isolation are massive problems in the modern world, and especially for the elderly who are more vulnerable. This isolation can further lead to depression and a sense of meaninglessness. Islam, in stark contrast to this, sets the expectation that we must care for our elderly, not abandon them in old people homes with strangers who don't really care for them. Where it is reported that 2 out of every 3 nursing staff have committed abuse over the past year.[141]

From a Godless perspective, there is very little motivation to sacrifice your time. As far as the atheist is concerned, you only have one life. If you give up your time now, you will not get that back. However, in Islam, this is not the case. Allah says:

> "So give your close relatives their due, as well as the poor and the [needy] traveller. That is best for those who seek the pleasure of Allah, and it is they who will be successful. Whatever loans you give, [only] seeking interest at the expense of people's wealth will not increase with Allah. But whatever charity you give, [only] seeking the pleasure of Allah—it is they whose reward will be multiplied."[142]

---

139   Ibid., 17:23-24
140   "Loneliness in Older People", *NHS*,
141   "Abuse of Older People", *World Health Organisation (WHO)*,
142   Ibid., 30:38-39

No deed ever goes wasted. Every sacrifice in this world is seen as an investment in the hereafter. It is impossible for the believer to feel like they are wasting their time by investing it in their parents; those who cared for them and provided for them in their youth. Having this duty on yourself is also a reassurance that this duty is something that will be passed on to your own children, and that you have the safety of care from those you love in your age as well. This sense of duty and commitment to each other, is again, a huge source of meaning and purpose for those that believe.

This sense of duty also rubs off onto the charitable acts of the believer, despite having less wealth on average, the data suggests that the Muslims are one of the most generous communities:

> "Muslims give more to charity than other religious groups, new research suggests. At almost £371 each, Muslims topped the poll of religious groups that give to charity. When they donated last year, atheists averaged £116, The Times reported (£). The ICM poll found that Jewish donors gave an average of £270 per person. Roman Catholics averaged just over £178, Christians just under £178 and Protestants £202."[143]

Not only are Muslims giving nearly double compared to other religious groups, but they are outdoing their atheist counterparts by more than 300%! And this is not just in international religious efforts. In fact, the data shows that the Muslims often give way more readily to their local communities, and are willing to give to both religious and non-religious causes:

> "Despite Islamophobic tropes suggesting that Muslim-Americans are more aligned to international causes, only 15 percent of their giving is focused on such causes while 85 percent of their gifts support American charitable causes. Despite being poorer than the average American household, Muslim-Americans participated in charitable giving and volunteering at higher levels than the average household.
>
> The survey finds that Muslims give more towards both faith-based causes and non-faith-based causes than non-Muslims. Overall, Muslim-Americans gave $3,200 for charitable giving compared to $1,905 for the general population."[144]

---

143 "Muslims 'Give Most to Charity', Ahead Of Christians, Jews And Atheists, Poll Finds", *The Huffington Post UK*, 3 October 2013,
144 "Muslim Americans: A Growing Force in Philanthropy", *Lilly Family School of Philanthropy*, 7 October 2021,

This level of charity really helps to build bonds within communities. The believer recognises they have a God given duty to their neighbours and the people around them. The recipients of this behaviour really do recognise this. I believe this is why Islam is one of the fastest growing religions in the world today. Not just because of birth rates (which it is), but also because of religious switching.[145] The Muslim community has a lot to offer in terms of their duties towards their wider community, and again, this has a huge impact on a sense of meaning and purpose in wider society. Everyone has a role to play, and it will not go unrewarded.

The list of those who the Muslims are responsible for is a long one. Allah makes this clear repeatedly in the Qur'an. In one example, He says:

> "Worship Allah [alone] and associate none with Him. And be kind to **parents, relatives, orphans, the poor, near and distant neighbours, close friends, [needy] travellers, and those [bondspeople] in your possession.** Surely Allah does not like whoever is arrogant, boastful, those who are stingy, promote stinginess among people, and withhold Allah's bounties. We have prepared for the disbelievers a humiliating punishment. Likewise, for those who spend their wealth to show off and do not believe in Allah or the Last Day. And whoever takes Satan as an associate—what an evil associate they have! What harm could have come to them if they had believed in Allah and the Last Day and donated from what Allah has provided for them? And Allah has [perfect] knowledge of them. Indeed, Allah never wrongs [anyone]—even by an atom's weight. And if it is a good deed, He will multiply it many times over and will give a great reward out of His grace."[146]

So, if you are looking for a sense of meaning and purpose, you will certainly find that in the bonds of Islam, and in the rights that Allah holds us to. For remember, not only are you to be dutiful to the above categories of people, but you will also fall into these categories and be the recipients of such kindness at some point in your life. You too, God willing, will be parents to children, relatives and friends to others, neighbours, and travellers. You will inevitably reap the benefits of these duties upon others and so it is a benefit the whole society can enjoy when it is something internalised by the populous.

---

145   "The Changing Global Religious Landscape", *Pew Research Centre*, 5 April 2017,

146   Qur'an, 4:36-40

A Solid Foundation for the Human Being

I now intend to show how Islam deals with Cosmic and Existential Nihilism. As a quick reminder of what these are, Cosmic Nihilism is the position that the Universe has no meaning and Existential Nihilism is that I as an individual (and any individual for that matter) have no meaning in life. Ultimately, I, like the universe, will inevitably perish. At base, the universe is cold and indifferent, and there is no higher purpose to it being arranged one way or another. It follows from this by greater reason that my own life is even more meaningless. My actions do not make a difference in the grand scheme of things, and I will eventually be forgotten; "For dust you *are*, and to dust you shall return."[147] Ultimately, no matter how significant I may think I am, it is all delusion. I do not matter because nothing matters. We previously went over several motivations for this mentality, so we will not go over that again now but rather focus on why Islam resolves this mentality.

If someone accepts Islam, it follows necessarily that both the universe and all of life have a purpose and a meaning. Allah reiterates this to us in the Qur'an repeatedly. Firstly, regarding the creation and in direct response to those who fall under the grasp of "nihilism", Allah says: "We have not created the heavens and earth and everything in between without purpose, as the disbelievers think".[148] If God exists and He is an eternal being who created everything in the universe for a reason, then it does not matter whether someone directly experiences that meaning. It would still objectively be the case that nihilism is false. Someone's sense of nihilism here would be completely misplaced and irrelevant to the facts. It is not just in this one verse that Allah makes this claim, there are many places. For example, elsewhere He also says the following:

---

147   The Bible, Genesis 3:19,
148   Qur'an, 38:27

> "We have not created the heavens and the earth and everything in between except for a purpose. And the Hour is certain to come, so forgive graciously."[149]

> "He is the One Who made the sun a radiant source and the moon a reflected light, with precisely ordained phases, so that you may know the number of years and calculation of time. Allah did not create all this except for a purpose. He makes the signs clear for people of knowledge."[150]

> "We did not create the heavens and the earth and everything in between for sport. We only created them for a purpose, but most of these (pagans) do not know."[151]

> "He created the heavens and the earth for a purpose. Exalted is He above what they associate with Him (in worship)."[152]

It is impossible to go into the state of believing in Allah, believe the Qur'an is His words, read this and then at the same time come to be a Cosmic Nihilist. These views are completely incompatible with one another. If Allah exists and the Qur'an is from Him, then we can be certain that this universe, and by extension, every individual in humanity is not the product of a random accident. What does Islam say about Existential Nihilism? Allah asks this question as well; He says: "Do people think they will be left without purpose?"[153] and: "Did you think We had created you in vain, and that you would not be brought back to Us?"[154] Again, the answer is given very succinctly, and we are assured of the following:

> "Have they not reflected upon their own being? Allah only created the heavens and the earth and everything in between for a purpose and an appointed term. Yet most people are truly in denial of the meeting with their Lord!"[155]

---

149   Ibid., 15:85
150   Ibid., 10:5
151   Ibid., 44:38-39
152   Ibid., 16:3
153   Ibid., 75:36
154   Ibid., 23:115
155   Ibid., 30:8

He even tells us what this purpose is, specifically, by explaining very clearly that He "did not create the jinn and mankind except that they may worship Me."[156] So we *do* have a purpose! If Allah exists, the Qur'an is the word of God and Muhammad ﷺ is His messenger, then as believers, we have absolutely no reason whatsoever to fall into a state of Existential Nihilism either. The only way this could occur is if we become disconnected from the teachings of Allah by ceasing to reflect on the principles and explanations given to us by Him. In the Qur'an, we are given a beautiful set of verses that express the attitude of a true believer, who has come to understand the necessity of the existence of our Creator:

> "To Allah (alone) belongs the kingdom of the heavens and the earth. And Allah is Most capable of everything. Indeed, in the creation of the heavens and the earth and the alternation of the day and night, there are signs for people of reason. (They are) those who remember Allah while standing, sitting, and lying on their sides, and reflect on the creation of the heavens and the earth (and pray), "Our Lord! You have not created (all of) this without purpose. Glory be to You! Protect us from the torment of the Fire."[157]

This perfectly expresses the ultimate consequences of belief in Allah and what He has sent down. Existence is not simply, at its foundation, just a bunch of atoms colliding with atoms and nothing else beyond that. This is the very attitude that is reiterated by the likes of Richard Dawkins when he said:

> "On the contrary, if the universe were just electrons and selfish genes, meaningless tragedies like the crashing of this bus are exactly what we should expect, along with equally meaningless good fortune. Such a universe would be neither evil nor good in intention. It would manifest no intentions of any kind. In a universe of blind physical forces and genetic replication, some people are going to get hurt, other people are going to get lucky, and you won't find any rhyme or reason in it, nor any justice. The universe we observe has precisely the properties we should expect if there is, at bottom, no design, no purpose, no evil and no good, nothing but blind, pitiless indifference."[158]

---

156   Ibid., 51:56
157   Ibid., 3:189-191
158   Dawkins R. & Ward L., *River Out of Eden: A Darwinian View of Life*, (London: Weidenfeld & Nicolson, 1995), pp. 132-133

This is the consequence of the beliefs of the new atheist types that do not believe in God and reduce everything to the material world, i.e., naturalism. However, if Allah exists and Islam is true, then it is not that the foundation of the universe is lifeless, cold, and indifferent to the concerns of mankind. It is not the case that Justice and concepts such as good and evil are completely meaningless words with reference to nothing but the delusions of man. If Justice is not attained in this life, it will certainly be attained in the hereafter, as promised by Al-'Adl (The Utterly Just), Al-Hakam (The Impartial Judge). Allah has created everything with a purpose and your ability or inability to see that cannot take away from this fact. Whether you are capable or incapable of recognising Allah's absolute existence and the truthfulness of the Prophets - and by extension, the truthfulness of Islam – it makes no difference to the fact of the matter that it is the case.

Furthermore, not only does belief in Islam guarantee a meaningful life, but we can also say that Allah understands His creation better than anyone. He gives us our religion, Islam, which offers a solid foundation that appeals to the natural state of the human being. Human beings need worship in their life, and if it isn't directed to God, it inevitably becomes directed to other things. In relation to this, it is interesting to know that the Qur'an does not acknowledge the existence of the "atheist". This is not to say there are not people out there who either deny his existence or refuse to acknowledge that He is worthy of worship. Rather, it is tied to the Islamic understanding of what worship is and how that worship can be directed to things besides Allah, rendering these things "gods"; whether this is done knowingly or unknowingly, and whether it is acknowledged or recognised by the one who participates in the worship or not.

So, what is worship in the Islamic sense? The disbelievers (and maybe even sometimes the believers) often assume that worship is restricted to things like the 5 daily prayers, or clear and obvious acts of devotion to something that is explicitly understood to be a God or gods, such as when the Christians put their hands together when they beseech Jesus, or the Buddhist's when they prostrate before large golden statues of men that lived less than 100 years ago.

But is that the case? According to Islamic doctrine, nearly everything can become worship if it is done for that which you value the most, which when properly done is for the sake of Allah (the one most worthy of worship). This means that if you give charity, smile, treat someone with kindness, or fulfil your duty towards them, and you do it for the pleasure of Allah, this has the potential to become an act of worship (when done sincerely with the correct intention). However, if you obey something else in disobedience to Allah (therefore taking them as an authority over God), to attain their pleasure or your own pleasure, then this can be construed as worshipping that *instead of God*. We see this very thing being displayed in Ibn Kathir's explanation of Chapter 9 verse 31 in the Qur'an, where he says:

> "Imam Ahmad, At-Tirmidhi and Ibn Jarir At-Tabari recorded a Hadith via several chains of narration, from Adi bin Hatim, may Allah be pleased with him, who became Christian during the time of Jahiliyyah. When the call of the Messenger of Allah reached his area, Adi ran away to Ash-Sham, and his sister and several of his people were captured. The Messenger of Allah freed his sister and gave her gifts. So, she went to her brother and encouraged him to become Muslim and to go to the Messenger of Allah.
>
> Adi, who was one of the chiefs of his people (the tribe of Tai') and whose father, Hatim At-Ta'i, was known for his generosity, went to Al-Madinah. When the people announced his arrival, Adi went to the Messenger of Allah wearing a silver cross around his neck. The Messenger of Allah recited this ayah; (They took their rabbis and their monks to be their lords besides Allah [9:31]).
>
> Adi commented, «I said, 'They did not worship them.'»
>
> The Prophet said, «Yes they did. They (rabbis and monks) prohibited the permissible for them (Christians and Jews) and made permissible the prohibited, and they obeyed them. This is how they worshipped them.»[159]

So, by obeying something in direct conflict with the commandments of Allah, you are in fact taking them to be more of an authority than God himself. If God says do not practice usury, describing it as evil, and then someone comes along and in contradiction to this says it is permissible, listening to them rather than to God makes it clear who and what is higher on your value hierarchy and considered more authoritative. This also applies to the atheist, who values their own pleasure and the achievement of their own desires over that which God commands; a result of them reducing His command to the product of fiction.

Value hierarchies are essentially the set of all the things that we value and do not value. This hierarchy forms a pyramid, at the top are the things we value the most, and at the bottom are the things we do not value at all. Ideally, Allah should be at the top of everyone's value hierarchy because He is the most perfect of all beings and is the only One who is in possession of the most perfect attributes. He is that which all of creation is dependent upon and He is the Sustainer of all things. It is He who is in control

---

159 Ibn Kathir, Tafsir of Qur'an 9:31,

of everything, and it is He who will determine your fate in the afterlife. It does not make sense to value anything above Him as there is nothing greater than Him. Allahu Akbar, one of the most famous Arabic sayings, (unfortunately having a negative connotation in the west), means God is Greater. We say that because it is true. Whatever exists, whatever you value more than Him, God IS Greater than it.

Now if you remove God from the top of your value hierarchy and value other things more than Him, He is not removed from the hierarchy completely. Remember, the value hierarchy is not just made up of the things you value, but also of the things you do not (they just end up further down towards the bottom of the pile). By not believing you are essentially valuing God less than other things. Allah says in the Qur'an: "Have you seen the one who has taken their own desires as their god?"[160] This is to say they value their desires more than anything else in existence. Is this not echoed in a very similar way by the likes of Nietzsche when he says:

> "God is dead! God remains dead! And we have killed him! How can we console ourselves, the murderers of all murderers! The holiest and the mightiest thing the world has ever possessed has bled to death under our knives: who will wipe this blood from us? With what water could we clean ourselves? What festivals of atonement, what holy games will we have to invent for ourselves? Is the magnitude of this deed not too great for us? Do we not ourselves have to become gods merely to appear worthy of it?"[161]

Is this not exactly what is happening? I cannot help but think about these grand festivals that mankind is now so eager to participate in. The altar has been replaced with a stage. The priests have been replaced with musicians who seek to bring their audience to a state of euphoria. They provide them with moving music, visual shows and lyrics which act as commandments and a guide for those who memorise them. The youth turn their bedrooms into shrines of their favourite artists, plastering their walls with posters and fan paraphernalia. They follow their idols on multiple social media platforms and are ready to defend them, absorbing what they say on political issues as though their tweets were stone tablets sent from The Divine. But what is it that these new prophets preach? What is the aqida (the beliefs) of the modernised human?

---

160   Qur'an, 25:43
161   Nietzsche F., *The Gay Science*, (Cambridge: Cambridge University Press, 2017), p. 120.

Individualism; YOLO; Live your life; Ignore the haters; You do you; Attain your desires and do not worry about what people think about you; Don't concern yourself with death or notions of the afterlife; Become your own gods! Go ahead and elevate your own desires to the top of your value hierarchies and reorient your life to revolve around achieving them! Nothing else! Stop having babies; they're too much of a sacrifice of your freedom and a burden to the world! Stop getting married! Who needs long-term committed relationships? It just stops you from experiencing new things and new people! Sex, drugs, and rock & roll! Anyone who tells you otherwise is a "dinosaur"!

It is often assumed that the modern world is somehow fundamentally unique. But the truth is, the issues we are currently dealing with today have been going on for millennia. Believers are often accused of following ancient practices as though this is enough to show it is wrong, while themselves referring to what they do as "natural" or "normal" because they find examples of it throughout history. These things were happening before the arrival of Islam and were being recognised in the Qur'an 1400 years ago. Allah is asking the audience of the revelation, the people at the time of the prophet ﷺ, to consider those who elevate their desires, their wants, to the highest status above what God commands. He asks them to see how this does in fact clearly resemble worship, and this is as relevant today as it ever has been throughout history. Humanity often finds itself stuck in a loop.

Worship is inescapable. Whatever it is that you show the most love, devote yourself to the most, venerate or honour more than anything else, you are essentially worshipping it. Either you worship God, or you worship other things. However, everything other than God inevitably turns to dust and ultimately relies on God as well. There is a brilliant quote from John Ortberg, where he perfectly expresses the fruitlessness of chasing the world. He says:

> "Now my grandmother was a wonderful person. She taught me how to play the game monopoly. She understood that the name of the game was to acquire. She would accumulate everything she could and eventually, she became the master of the board. And eventually, every time, she would take my last dollar and I would quit in utter defeat. And then she would always say the same thing to me. She'd look at me and she'd say: «One day you'll learn to play the game.»
>
> One summer I played monopoly with a neighbour, almost every day, all day long, we'd play monopoly for hours. And that summer I learned to play the game. I came to understand the

only way to win is to make a total commitment to acquisition. I came to understand that money and possessions, that's the way that you keep score. And by the end of that summer, I was more ruthless than my grandmother. I was ready to bend the rules if I had to, to win that game. And I sat down with her to play that fall. I took everything she had. I destroyed her financially and psychologically. I watched her give her last dollar and quit in utter defeat.

And then she had one more thing to teach me. Then she said: "Now it all goes back in the box. All those houses and hotels, all the railroads and utility companies. All that property and all that wonderful money, now it all goes back in the box." I didn‹t want it to go back in the box. "No" she said, "none of it was really yours. You got a little heated up about it for a while. But it was around a long time before you sat down at the board, and it will be here after you're gone; players come, and players go. But it all goes back in the box. Houses and cars, titles and clothes, filled barns, bulging portfolios, even your body! Because the fact is, that everything I clutch and consume, and hoard, is going to go back in the box and I›m going to lose it all. There's not much of an ROI[162] on that.

So, you have to ask yourself, when you finally get that ultimate promotion, when you've made the ultimate purchase, when you buy the ultimate home, when you have stored up financial security and climbed the ladder of success to the highest rung you can possibly climb it, and the thrill wears off, and it will wear off… THEN WHAT?? How far do you have to walk down that road before you see where it leads? Surely you understand it will never be enough! So you have to ask yourself the question: WHAT MATTERS?"[163]

Ultimately, what use is there in collecting water with a sieve? We fight and clamber over the things of this world, but to what end? Black Friday arrives every year, and like a flock of vultures around a rotting corpse, we fight and push each other aside to get our hands on some slightly discounted goods. We work ourselves to the bone to accrue enough capital so we can afford our next holiday to Ibiza or Tenerife, where we blast £5,000 in a couple of weeks of craziness that we can barely remember. We invest hours of our time to build palaces in Minecraft. We do all of this for what exactly? For brief moments of pleasure which always wear off? Is that it? Where is

---

162   (Return of interest)
163   For those of you who have not heard this in spoken word, I really recommend looking for the video on YouTube and giving it a listen: Ortberg J.,"The Monopoly of Life – It all goes back in the box", *theJourneyofPurpose TJOP,* YouTube,

the purpose in any of this? If there is no purpose to this life beyond these pointless things, why bother with life at all?

This is the very question that existential philosophers tried to answer in the aftermath of Nietzsche's work. If nihilism is to be affirmed, as many of them were beginning to believe it should be after the "death of God", how are we (collectively or individually) supposed to come back from that? Is life worth living at all if this is the case? Is this not a fundamental question that everyone who falls into nihilism should be asking? Albert Camus, a famous French-Algerian philosopher, stressed the question of suicide as being the most fundamental question of all:

> "There is but one truly serious philosophical problem and that is suicide. **Judging whether life is or is not worth living amounts to answering the fundamental question of philosophy.** All the rest – whether the world has three dimensions, whether the mind has nine or twelve categories – comes afterwards. These are games; one must first answer. And if it is true, as Nietzsche claims, that a philosopher, to deserve our respect, must preach by example, you can appreciate the importance of that reply, for it will precede the definitive act. These are facts the heart can feel; yet they call for careful study before they become clear to the intellect.
>
> If I ask myself how to judge that this question is more urgent than that, I reply that one judges by the actions it entails. I have never seen anyone die for the ontological argument. Galileo who held a scientific truth of great importance abjured it with the greatest ease as soon as it endangered his life. In a certain sense, he did right. That truth was not worth the stake. Whether the earth or the sun revolves around the other is a matter of profound indifference. To tell the truth, it is a futile question. On the other hand, I see many people die because they judge that life is not worth living. I see others paradoxically getting killed for the ideas or illusions that give them a reason for living (what is called a reason for living is also an excellent reason for dying). **I therefore conclude that the meaning of life is the most urgent of questions.**"[164]

So, is life worth living? Is this not fundamentally one of the most important things we should be thinking about? Who should really care among the layman about Emmanuel Kant's Critique of Pure Reason and the "Synthetic a priori"? What use is this information to the average person if it offers no

---

164   Camus A., *The Myth of Sisyphus*, (London: Penguin Books, 2005), p 1.

hope of answering what the meaning of life is? Who cares about arbitrary scientific facts if we cannot link this to a reason for living?

Life is a strange thing; today especially. We have more than we can ever have expected our ancestors to dream of. Me, and many people in the modern world, have so much to be grateful for. Even many of the poorest among us are surrounded by many luxuries.

As I have already mentioned, I grew up in a rough area of North Manchester, England. We were not rich. My dad was in and out of prison, and when he wasn't locked up, he was battling his heroin addiction. My mum worked for minimum wages as a waitress, and we lived off her tips. Our family lived in Poland and Scotland, so for the most part we were alone without much support. My dad's drug addiction ate up a lot of our cash, and we got by with whatever my mum could provide. My mum struggled a lot to provide for us. Even then, we still had a lot to be grateful for. We had clean running water that you could drink straight from the tap. We had hot water, and our home was heated. We had food on our plates and very rarely went hungry. We had access to chocolate and sweets, fizzy drinks, and fruit from all over the world. We had a free education, health care and access to public transport. We had a washing machine and fridge freezer. As poor as we were, we lived better than kings did 100 years ago. We had a lot.

My great grandmother would have had to clean the families' clothes by hand on a wash board for hours. They would have had to heat the home using fires with wood they collected from the forest. They would have had to wash themselves with cold water. Compared to our ancestors, we have it a lot easier in many ways. But despite all of this, we, the modern people, still suffer. In 1 year in the UK (2017-2018) 7.3 million people were taking antidepressants, which is 17% of the adult population; nearly 1 in every 5 people![165] These are people who very likely had access to food, running water, clothing, and heating, but what they did not have was a sense that life was worth living as they were unfortunately unable to find any meaning in it. However, here I have presented to you Islam. A complete way of life that appeals to the rational and spiritual aspects of the human being. It offers you a community of people who have a sense of duty and care towards you, and it infuses your life with meaning, regardless of what you're going through!

---

165 Department of Health and Social Care (UK) n.d, "Prescribed Medicines Review Summary", HM Government,

Conclusion

Islam is a viable solution because it provides meaning! It offers a way of life that is fulfilling and in line with our innate disposition, given to us by God. It affirms that the universe and our lives most certainly have a purpose, and that Allah does not create things in jest. This life is not random and pointless, but rather it is divinely created and infused with significance. It is a test, to determine who among us is worthy of something great in the hereafter, and who is worthy of punishment. The Qur'an is a letter from God to you, to read; so read it! In it we find guidance which helps to protect us from many of the things that plague the most vulnerable in society today. It provides you with a reason to wake up in the morning, and to continue throughout the day. It has the potential to transform everything you do into an act of worship for the One who made you, who is most worthy of that worship. It provides us with duties that we must fulfil, and we are at the same time, recipients of the very same duties. It offers entry to a new family, a new community, and you will find yourself loving a stranger simply because you share a love for Allah and His messenger ﷺ. It gives practical guidance from the very bottom to the very top. Kings and rulers are subject to the same law as the farmer. This is a religion that softened the hearts of many, including the likes of Malcolm X. A man who at one point was a hard separationist and could not see any possibility of the races living together in peace *until* he went on Hajj and saw what Islam was capable of with his own eyes![166]

Islam continues to grow to this day at the fastest rates of any other religion, and not just by birth-rates, but also by conversion.[167] Islam is going to play a key role in the future, and I truly believe it makes perfect sense to step on the path of seeking knowledge about one of the greatest ways of life

---

166 Malcolm X, 'Malcolm X Pleased by Whites' Attitude On Trip to Mecca', *The New York* Times, 8 May 1964, p.1
167 Pew Research Centre, 'The Changing Global Religious Landscape', *Pew Research Centre*, 5 April 2017,

the world has ever seen. I hope and pray that this book has played a part in helping you see this, and at least opened your hearts to the possibility of investigating it further.

Peace and blessings upon you all. May you find truth and order in this increasingly false and chaotic world.

Bibliography

"Abuse of Older People", *World Health Organisation (WHO)*, , accessed 12 March 2023

Alcohol Change UK, 'Alcohol Statistics', *Alcohol Change UK,* <https://alcoholchange.org.uk/alcohol-facts/fact-sheets/alcohol-statistics>, accessed 17 January 2021

Alkiek T., "Religious Minorities Under Muslim Rule", *Yaqeen Institute for Islamic Research*, 8 Feb 2017, <https://yaqeeninstitute.org/tesneem-alkiek/religious-minorities-under-muslim-rule>, accessed 28 May 2021

Anthony, A., 'Sam Harris, the new atheist with a spiritual side', *The Guardian*, 16 February 2019, <https://www.theguardian.com/books/2019/feb/16/sam-harris-interview-new-atheism-four-horsemen-faith-science-religion-rationalism>, accessed 17 January 2021

The Bible, Genesis 3:19, <https://www.biblehub.com/genesis/3-19.htm>, accessed 13 March 2023

Bican Şahin, *Toleration: The Liberal Virtue*, (Lexington Books, 2010)

Bloom P., 'Religion is natural', Developmental *Science*, 10/1, (2007), 147-151

Britannica, The Editors of Encyclopaedia. 'Nihilism'. *Encyclopedia Britannica*, 13 Mar. 2020, <https://www.britannica.com/topic/nihilism>, accessed 5 February 2021.

Britannica, The Editors of Encyclopaedia. "Reformation". Encyclopedia Britannica, 2 Dec. 2022, https://www.britannica.com/event/Reformation. Accessed 12 March 2023.

Camus A., *The Myth of Sisyphus*, (London: Penguin Books, 2005).

Data Commons Team, 'Data Commons Timeline: London Population', *Data commons,* <https://datacommons.org/tools/timeline#&place=nuts/UKI&statsVar=Count_Person>, accessed 17 January 2021.

Dawkins R., "Richard Dawkins: Faith | Big Think", *Big Think*, 2 June 2011, YouTube, <https://youtu.be/Sm22oQ5wks4>, access 11 May 2021

Dawkins R. & Ward L., *River Out of Eden: A Darwinian View of Life*, (London: Weidenfeld & Nicolson, 1995)

de Botton A., "How Science Could – at Last – Properly Replace Religion", *The School of Life*, <https://www.theschooloflife.com/thebookoflife/how-science-could-at-last-properly-replace-religion/>, accessed 18 July 2020

Department of Health and Social Care (UK) n.d, "Prescribed Medicines Review Summary", HM Government, https://www.gov.uk/government/publications/prescribed-medicines-review-report/prescribed-medicines-review-summary, accessed 13 March 2023

Descartes R., *The Philosophical Writings of Descartes: Volume II*, Trans. By Cottingham J., Stoothoff R., & Murdoch D., (Cambridge: Cambridge University Press, 1999).

Donelson R, 'The Nihilist', *The Pragmatism and Prejudice of Oliver Wendell Holmes Jr.*, Edited by Vannatta S., (Maryland: Lexington Books, 2019), https://core.ac.uk/download/pdf/227471592.pdf, accessed 10 May 2023

Elsworthy E., 'More than half of Britons describe their neighbours as 'strangers'', *Independent*, 29 May 2018, <https://www.independent.co.uk/news/uk/home-news/britons-neighbours-strangers-uk-community-a8373761.html>, accessed 17 January 2021

Enfield N., "We're in a post-truth world with eroding trust and accountability." *The Guardian Newspaper*, 16 November 2017, <https://www.theguardian.com/commentisfree/2017/nov/17/were-in-a-post-truth-world-with-eroding-trust-and-accountability-it-cant-end-well>, accessed 16 January 2021

"Faith", Dictionary.com, 2023, https://www.dictionary.com/browse/faith, accessed 12 March 2023

"Faith", Cambridge Dictionary, Cambridge University Press, <https://dictionary.cambridge.org/dictionary/english/faith>, accessed 12 March 2023

Frankl V. E., *Man's Search for Meaning*, (London: Rider, 2004)

Gertz N., *Nihilism and Technology*, (London: Rowman & Littlefield International LTD, 2018)

Harry M. Bracken, *Descartes* (Oxford: Oneworld Publications, 2002)

Harvard Health Publishing, 'Giving thanks can make you happier', *Harvard Medical School*, November 2011, <https://www.health.harvard.edu/healthbeat/giving-thanks-can-make-you-happier>, accessed 17 January 2021

Heidegger M., *Being & Time*, (Oxford: Blackwell Publishing LTD, 2016)

Heisel, M.J. & Flett, G.L., "Purpose in Life, Satisfaction with Life, and Suicide Ideation in a Clinical Sample", *Journal of Psychopathology and Behavioral Assessment*, 26/127, (2004)

Hidaka B. H., "Depression as a Disease of Modernity: Explanations for Increasing Prevalence.", *Journal of Affective Disorders*, 140/3 (2012), <https://www.ncbi.nlm.nih.gov/pmc/articles/PMC3330161/>, accessed 16 January 2021

Ibn Kathir, Tafsir of Qur'an 9:31, <https://quran.com/en/9:30/tafsirs/en-tafisr-ibn-kathir>, accessed 13 March 2023

"In U.S., Decline of Christianity Continues at Rapid Pace", *Pew Research Center*, 17 October 2019, <https://www.pewforum.org/2019/10/17/in-u-s-decline-of-christianity-continues-at-rapid-pace/>, accessed 17 January 2021

Kurzgesagt – In a Nutshell, "Optimistic Nihilism", 26 July 2017, <https://youtu.be/MBRquoYOH14?t=225>, accessed 18 July 2020,

Large W., *Heidegger's Being and Time*, (Edinburgh: Edinburgh University Press, 2008)

Lawton G., "The God issue: Alain de Botton's religion for atheists", *NewScientist*, 14 March 2012, <https://www.newscientist.com/article/mg21328562-400-the-god-issue-alain-de-bottons-religion-for-atheists/#ixzz6SpE9LnKB> accessed 21 July 2020

Lings M., *Muhammad: his life based on the earliest sources*, (Cambridge: The Islamic Text Society, 2017),

"Loneliness in Older People", *NHS*, https://www.nhs.uk/mental-health/feelings-symptoms-behaviours/feelings-and-symptoms/loneliness-in-older-people/, accessed 12 March 2023

Malcolm X, 'Malcolm X Pleased By Whites' Attitude On Trip to Mecca', *The New York Times*, 8 May 1964, <https://www.nytimes.com/1964/05/08/archives/malcolm-x-pleased-by-whites-attitude-on-trip-to-mecca.html>, accessed 17 January 2021

Matheson D., 'Incoherence of Soft Nihilism', *Think*, 47/16, (2017) 127-135 (p.127)

Merriam-Webster, 'Value', *Merriam-Webster Dictionary*, <https://www.merriam-webster.com/dictionary/value>, accessed 16 January 2021

"Muslim Americans: A Growing Force in Philanthropy", *Lilly Family School of Philanthropy*, 7 October 2021, https://philanthropy.iupui.edu/news-events/philanthropy-matters/2021-issues/october-2021.html#muslimgiving, accessed 12 March 2023

"Muslims 'Give Most To Charity', Ahead Of Christians, Jews And Atheists, Poll Finds", *The Huffington Post UK*, 3 October 2013, https://www.huffingtonpost.co.uk/2013/07/21/muslims-give-most_n_3630830.html, accessed 12 March 2023.

Nagel T., 'The Absurd', *The Journal of Philosophy*, 68/20, (1971), 716-727,

Nietzsche F., *The Anti-Christ: A Criticism of Christianity*, trans. By A.M. Ludovici, (New York; Barnes & Noble, 2006)

Nietzsche F., *The Will to Power*, (London: Penguin Group, 2017) p. 15,

Nietzsche F., *The Gay Science*, (Cambridge: Cambridge University Press, 2017)

Nietzsche F., *Twilight of the Idols*, (Oxford: Oxford University Press, 2008)

Nietzsche F., *The Will to Power*, (UK: Penguin Books, 2017)

Ortberg J.,"The Monopoly of Life – It all goes back in the box", *theJourneyofPurpose TJOP*, YouTube, <https://www.youtube.com/watch?v=kSAVN-nYSLI>, accessed 13 March 2023

"Political Polarization in the American Public, Section 1: Growing Ideological Consistency", *Pew Research Centre*, 12 June 2014, <https://www.pewresearch.org/politics/2014/06/12/section-1-growing-ideological-consistency/>, accessed 17 January 2021

"Public Trust in Government: 1958-2019", *Pew Research Centre*, 11 April 2019, <https://www.pewresearch.org/politics/2019/04/11/public-trust-in-government-1958-2019/>, accessed 19 July 2020

Phenix P. H., *Realms of Meaning*, (New York: McGraw-Hill Book Company, 1964)

Plato, *The Republic*, Trans. By D. Lee, (London: Penguin Books, 2007),

Rogan J. & Dawkins R., '#1366 - Richard Dawkins', *The Joe Rogan Experience*, 21 October 2019,

Ruse M., 'Dawkins et al bring us into disrepute', *The Guardian*, 2 November 2009, <https://www.theguardian.com/commentisfree/belief/2009/nov/02/atheism-dawkins-ruse>, accessed 17 January 2021

Schopenhauer A., *The Essays of Arthur Schopenhauer: Studies in Pessimism*, Vol. 4, Trans. By T. Bailey Saunders, (Pennsylvania: The Pennsylvania State University, 2005)

Schwartz B., "The Paradox of Choice | Barry Schwartz", *TED*, 16 January 2007, <https://youtu.be/VO6XEQIsCoM?t=1010>, accessed 17 January 2021,

Schwartz B., *The Paradox of Choice: Why More Is Less*, (New York: HarperCollins Publishers Inc., 2016)

Shilling A., 'Famous Liars in Greek Mythology', *Classroom synonym*, <https://classroom.synonym.com/famous-liars-greek-mythology-21981.html>, accessed 16 January 2021

Snowden C., "Alcohol and the Public Purse: Do drinkers pay their way?", IEA Discussion Paper No.63, *Institute of Economic Affairs*, < https://iea.org.uk/wp-content/uploads/2016/07/DP_Alcohol%20and%20the%20public%20purse_63_amended2_web.pdf>, accessed 12 March 2023.

Stang, Nicholas F., "Kant's Transcendental Idealism", *The Stanford Encyclopedia of Philosophy* (Winter 2022 Edition), Edward N. Zalta & Uri Nodelman (eds.), <https://plato.stanford.edu/archives/win2022/entries/kant-transcendental-idealism/>. Accessed 12 March 2023

"The Changing Global Religious Landscape", *Pew Research Centre*, 5 April 2017, <https://assets.pewresearch.org/wp-content/uploads/sites/11/2017/04/07092755/FULL-REPORT-WITH-APPENDIXES-A-AND-B-APRIL-3.pdf> , accessed 17 January 2021

The Clear Qur'an, Trans by Dr M. Khattab, <https://quran.com>, accessed 8 February 2021,

The Holy Bible, English Standard Version, <https://www.biblegateway.com/>, accessed 8 February 2021

Toffler A., *Future Shock* (New York: Random House Inc., 1971)

Turner J., "Who Shoulders the Burden of Proof? Reformed Epistemology & Properly Basic Islamic Belief", *Sapience Institute*, 9 December 2020, <https://sapienceinstitute.org/who-shoulders-the-burden-of-proof-reformed-epistemology-and-properly-basic-islamic-belief/>, accessed 17 January 2021

Tzortzis H. A., *The Divine Reality: God, Islam & The Mirage of Atheism*, (Lion Rock Publishing, 2019)

World Health Organisation, 'Mental Health and Substance Use', *WHO*, <https://www.who.int/mental_health/prevention/suicide/suicideprevent/en/>, accessed 16 January 2021

World Health Organisation (WHO), 'Suicide', *WHO*, 2 Sept. 2019, <https://www.who.int/news-room/fact-sheets/detail/suicide>, accessed 16 January 2021

Zakariya A., *The Forbidden Prophecies,* (London: One Reason, 2019)

Zakariya A., *The Eternal Challenge: A Journey Through the Miraculous Qur'an*, (London: One Reason, 2015)

Hadith

Sunan al-Tirmidhi 3334, <https://sunnah.com/urn/680450>, accessed 12 March 2023.

Sahih al-Bukhari 107, https://sunnah.com/bukhari:107, accessed 12 March 2023

Sahih al-Bukhari 7499, < https://sunnah.com/bukhari:7499>, accessed 12 March 2023

Sahih Muslim 2607c, < https://sunnah.com/muslim:2607c>, accessed 12 March 2023

Jami' at-Tirmidhi 2646, < https://sunnah.com/tirmidhi:2646>, accessed 12 March 2023

Sahih al-Bukhari 5641, https://sunnah.com/bukhari:5641, accessed 12 March 2023

Jami' at-Tirmidhi 2398, < https://sunnah.com/tirmidhi:2398>, accessed 12 March 2023

Sahih Muslim 2999, < https://sunnah.com/muslim:2999>, accessed 12 March 2023

Sunan Ibn Majah 181, <https://sunnah.com/ibnmajah:181>, accessed 12 March 2023

Riyad as-Salihin 461, https://sunnah.com/riyadussalihin:461, accessed 12 March 2023

Sahih al-Bukhari 7498, < https://sunnah.com/bukhari:7498>, accessed 12 March 2023

Al-Mu'jam al-Awsat 7073, <https://www.abuaminaelias.com/dailyhadithonline/2016/02/12/sent-prophet-perfect-good-deeds/>, accessed 12 March 2023